W9-ASD-561

DISCARD

No Longer the Property of
New Castle County

Praise for

The Cost of My Faith

"Jack Phillips is a very courageous and patriotic American who is a splendid example of what it will take to preserve the freedoms that we so often take for granted in this country. The reader of this book will quickly realize that God never sent you into a battle without equipping you to win. We cannot be the land of the free if we are not the home of the brave."

—**Benjamin S. Carson Sr.**, M.D., former United States
Secretary of Housing and Urban Development

"Inspired by Civil War leadership examples, Jack Phillips boldly stepped out in faith and launched his now-legendary Masterpiece Cakeshop. His dazzling artistry has included a bust of Denver Broncos quarterback John Elway and a portrait of Billy Graham, but he will forever be known as the creative genius who lived out his faith with kindness toward all while faithfully honoring biblical principles as a man of conscience. He will cheerfully serve one and all in 'an environment in which anyone and everyone could feel welcome.' But he will not violate his deeply held beliefs or convey a message through artistic creations that runs afoul of conscience. An instructional saga revealing modern-day challenges to our constitutional order, Jack Phillips's important book is an inspiring modern-day profile in courageous servanthood."

—**Ken Starr,** former president of Baylor University

"My friend Jack Phillips is an easygoing man, but that doesn't mean he hides his light under a bushel basket in the midst of darkness. Jack is living the Christian life as Scripture describes: 'As bold as a lion' (Proverbs 28:1). His book lays out a journey that has taken him from his Masterpiece Cakeshop in Colorado all the way to the U.S. Supreme Court in Washington, D.C. You will be amazed by his story and encouraged to see why God often allows trouble to come knocking. Jack's personal experience caused him to see that while society may be hostile to Christ's message, God uses it to give extraordinary platforms from which to testify to His power and His great salvation, often leading us along pathways we never would have sought. There is a cost for freedom, and Jesus ultimately paid the greatest price to win the souls of mankind. This book will open your eyes to the cost of your faith and the hope that Christ gives."

—**Franklin Graham,** president and CEO of the Billy Graham Evangelistic Association and Samaritan's Purse

"Take it from a family that knows what it's like to have people come after you for your beliefs: the only way you survive attacks on faith in our culture is to stand firm in Jesus Christ. Jack Phillips knows what it's like to pay a cost for his beliefs, and he shares his amazing story in *The Cost of My Faith*. We pray that reading this book, you will be inspired as much as we were."

—**Phil and Kay Robertson,** *New York Times* bestselling author (Phil) of *The Theft of America's Soul*

"To meet Jack Phillips is to meet a meek and loving man of God. His story in *The Cost of My Faith* relays his love for everyone and his conviction in Jesus Christ and the Holy Scriptures. We encourage you to read this book, follow this man's example, and be challenged to pay your cost for the kingdom of God when the moment arrives."

—**Al and Lisa Robertson,** co-authors of *Desperate Forgiveness*

"My friend Jack Phillips just wants to serve others and honor God through his business. But when he chose not to use his creative skills to celebrate something that violates his biblical convictions, he paid a heavy price. Jack took a courageous stand, and by not backing down, he became a modern-day hero of the faith. Now he's captured his story in this inspiring book. Jack's account has lessons for us all in today's culture. It's a must-read!"

—**Jim Daly,** president of Focus on the Family

"The author of Hebrews says about the faithful, some identified by name and others identified by only deed, that 'of whom the world was not worthy.' With quiet strength, Jack Phillips has loved both God and neighbor through a series of trials and tribulations, lawsuits and lost business, that would do in most of us. His story is a defining one of our time. It needed to be told, and it now has been in this great book, *The Cost of My Faith*. The implications of Jack's story must be reckoned with."

—**John Stonestreet,** host of *BreakPoint* and president of the Colson Center

"Jack Phillips's book begins as a great American story: hard work and hard-won lessons in Middle America. But Jack, an average American small-business owner, was attacked by massive forces that tried to destroy his livelihood and his reputation. This book is a testimony to Jack's faith in Christ and an opportunity for Him to share the Good News. A must-read!"

—**Eric Patterson,** Ph.D., executive vice president of the Religious Freedom Institute

"Jack Phillips is a soft-spoken, sensitive, humble man of great integrity. You cannot help loving him as he reflects God's love to all people he meets. Jack is also an artist—but not in ways you might expect. His 'canvas' is the beautiful cakes he designs, sculpts, and 'paints' with radiant colors to help people celebrate momentous events in their lives. Jack's cakes are indeed Masterpieces. But what is of preeminent importance to Jack is that he is a follower of Jesus. It was Jack's expression of his love for God's Word in a brief encounter with two men who wanted Jack to create a wedding cake that led him on the journey he describes in his book, *The Cost of My Faith*. It is the story of Jack's unwavering faith that sustained him during his long battle to exercise his constitutional rights and honor God. Jack's book will challenge you in your own journey of faith as well."

—**Michael J. Norton,** former Colorado United States Attorney

"Jack Phillips never intended to be a cultural warrior. But what are ordinary Christians to do in extraordinary times? *The Cost of My Faith* is Jack's story that includes both courage and conviction. The book has additional benefits for every person who values personal freedom, religious freedom, and artistic expression. Those benefits include inspiration, instruction, and encouragement. There may come a time when you might need to make a hard choice, a costly choice, a sacrificial choice, because you believe in immutable principles. Jack's story might be your story in the not too distant future."

—**Pastor Gino Geraci,** Salem Media talk show host and
president and founder of Scripture Says

"From God meeting Jack in an old blue '66 Mustang, through all the ups and downs of starting his own business, to facing death threats, and eventually a six-year battle to a U.S. Supreme Court victory, *The*

Cost of My Faith is the story of God's faithfulness to use an obedient man. Because of Jack Phillips, religious freedom is strengthened and America's future is brighter.

"America's success is because average men and women are courageous enough to stand strong for our founding principles. Jack Phillips faced tremendous hostility because of his religious values, responded with compassion and love, and God used all of it to make our country stronger. *The Cost of My Faith* is a must-read for all Americans!

"*The Cost of My Faith* is a behind-the-scenes look at America's most famous baker. The challenges he faced, the compassion and love he showed his persecutors, and the victory he had at the U.S. Supreme Court. Most importantly, the book provides insight into Jack's testimony. How God met him in an old blue '66 Mustang, and has been a constant presence in his life ever since."

—**Jeffrey Hunt,** director of the Centennial Institute at
Colorado Christian University

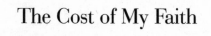

The Cost of My Faith

The Cost of My Faith

HOW A DECISION IN MY CAKE SHOP TOOK ME TO THE SUPREME COURT

Jack Phillips

SALEM
BOOKS

an imprint of Regnery Publishing
Washington, D.C.

Copyright © 2021 by Jack Phillips

All rights reserved. No part of this publication may be reproduced or transmitted in any form or by any means electronic or mechanical, including photocopy, recording, or any information storage and retrieval system now known or to be invented, without permission in writing from the publisher, except by a reviewer who wishes to quote brief passages in connection with a review written for inclusion in a magazine, newspaper, website, or broadcast.

Unless otherwise marked, all scriptures are taken from the NEW KING JAMES VERSION.® Copyright © 1982 by Thomas Nelson, Inc. Used by permission. All rights reserved.

Scriptures marked ESV are taken from THE HOLY BIBLE, ENGLISH STANDARD VERSION.® Copyright © 2001 by Crossway, a publishing ministry of Good News Publishers. Used by permission.

Scriptures marked KJV are taken from the KING JAMES VERSION, public domain.

Scriptures marked NASB are taken from the NEW AMERICAN STANDARD BIBLE®. Copyright © 1960, 1962, 1963, 1968, 1971, 1972, 1973, 1975, 1977, 1995 by the Lockman Foundation. Used by permission.

Scriptures marked NIV are taken from THE HOLY BIBLE, NEW INTERNATIONAL VERSION.® Copyright © 1973, 1978, 1984, 2011 by Biblica, Inc.™ Used by permission of Zondervan.

Scriptures marked NLT are taken from the HOLY BIBLE, NEW LIVING TRANSLATION. Copyright © 1996, 2004, 2007 by Tyndale House Foundation. Used by permission of Tyndale House Publishers, Inc., Carol Stream, Illinois, 60188. All rights reserved.

Salem Books™ is a trademark of Salem Communications Holding Corporation

Regnery® is a registered trademark of Salem Communications Holding Corporation

ISBN: 978-1-68451-080-1
eISBN: 978-1-68451-099-3

Library of Congress Control Number: 2020948297

Published in the United States by
Salem Books
An Imprint of Regnery Publishing
A Division of Salem Media Group
Washington, D.C.
www.SalemBooks.com

Manufactured in the United States of America

10 9 8 7 6 5 4 3 2 1

Books are available in quantity for promotional or premium use. For information on discounts and terms, please visit our website: www.SalemBooks.com.

I gladly dedicate this book to my wife, Debi.

Her love, perseverance, and patience throughout these years (all of these years, not just the years of the legal battles) has been an amazing evidence of God's grace in our lives. She has stood behind me, and, more importantly, she has stood beside me and supported and loved me through good times and—thankfully— through the times where I have definitely not been worth the energy and patience.

Contents

Prologue

Twenty seconds.

And one decision.

That's all it took to change my life forever. To turn the lives of my family members upside down, transform the future of my business, and even impact the laws of my country.

Because of those few seconds—and that one decision—I've gone from being a quiet cake artist with a strip-mall cake shop in the Denver suburb of Lakewood to an unlikely public figure who has been interviewed by national journalists, grilled by the women of *The View*, and judged and psychoanalyzed by countless men and women around kitchen tables and watercoolers all over America. I've had my life threatened, my name defamed, and my deepest beliefs judged by the Supreme Court of the United States.

And yet, that one decision was really only one in a long line of decisions—some of which seemed pretty critical at the moment, some of which did not—that together have brought my life to where it is today and prepared me for all the decisions I have yet to make.

For me, this book is my way of revisiting some of those decisions…in part, to better understand why I made them and to more fully realize their impact on my own life and on the lives of so many others. But I'm also hoping that this book may help you as you come to terms with some of the most important and far-reaching decisions of your own life—and as you try to prepare for what may turn out to be even more important choices still to come.

None of us, after all, know what's coming around the corner in these days of escalating social conflict and violence. (There's an old saying that "it's hard to predict things—especially the future.") I used to think, *What can happen? I've got my family, my friends, a good job, food on the table, a nice place to live.*

But that was before those twenty seconds.

And that one decision.

In the Bible, Jesus warned His disciples that they are headed into dangerous, uncharted territory. "I send you out as sheep in the midst of wolves," He said.[1] And after the last few years, I feel like I know what He meant.

But thankfully, He adds this assurance:

> You will be brought before governors and kings for My sake, as a testimony to them…but when they deliver you up, do not worry about how or what you should speak. For it will be given to you *in that hour* what you should speak; for it is not you who speak, but the Spirit of your Father who speaks in you.[2] (emphasis mine)

I can testify now to the truth of that promise. Because of one decision, I have stood "before governors and kings." And time after time, He has given me the words to say.

I wrote this book in part for my children and grandchildren, so they would have my record of what happened and some sense of how I felt while it was happening. I also wrote it for all of those who are curious about the truth behind what I said, what I meant, and what I've experienced in the crowded years since.

Fair warning as you read: I quote a lot of Bible verses—not to sound holier than thou, but because those verses are the foundation upon which I've built my beliefs, my attitude, and my life. I didn't do or say anything worth remembering on my own, and I didn't make my decisions in a vacuum. This book is my testimony of how God led me, decision by decision, to where I am today.

It's not the whole story, of course, any more than the gospels tell us the whole story of all that Jesus said and did in His time on the earth.[3] "Jesus did many other miraculous signs in the presence of His disciples," the Bible says, "but these are written so that you may believe that Jesus is the Christ, the Son of God, and that by believing, you may have life in His name."[4]

That's the main reason I've written this book: to share some of what God has done in my life, so that you may trust Him for what He wants to do in yours. You have your own talents, your own circumstances, your own opportunities to make decisions. I believe God wants to bless you, lead you, and help you with all of those things, as surely as He has for me.

The Bible tells us how some of the Apostle Paul's decisions led him to stand before kings—actual kings—with whom he shared his life story. One king, Agrippa, after hearing Paul's testimony, said, "You almost persuade me to be a Christian." To which Paul replied, "I would to God that not only you, but also all who hear me today, might become both almost and altogether such as I am, except for these chains."[5]

That's how I feel in writing this book. I wish everyone who reads it could know God's love as clearly as I do—but without having to be condemned by your state government officials or to spend most of a decade defending your beliefs.

If you are already a follower of Christ—and even if you aren't— there's a good chance He's leading you to some unknown places too.

To some unpredictable situations. To choices whose impact you can hardly imagine.

I hope this book will be a blessing to you, a help and encouragement to you, as you make those coming decisions.

1

The Conversation That Changed My Life

It was a hot and typically unpredictable July afternoon—the kind that can build into severe thunderstorms, hail, or just sunshine and straight-up heat on Colorado's Front Range. For me, this particular afternoon would bring both. And I wouldn't even have to go outside; today's heat and storms came from the wedding desk.

As usual, I was in the back part of my shop with my hands full baking, icing, and setting up cakes to be decorated, so my daughter Lisa and another female employee were taking care of customers up at the counter. At some point, I glanced up to see how things were going out front, and one of the women caught my eye. She nodded toward the wedding desk.

That is where I meet with couples looking to order something special in the way of wedding cakes—something carefully, creatively designed to delight their guests and communicate a message about their relationship. About twenty cakes were on display there to give customers an idea of how my imagination and artistry could bring their ideas and requests to life.

Two men were seated at the desk. One of our portfolios was open in front of them.

I slipped around the counter and into my seat behind the desk, ready to greet them.

"I'm David," said the gentleman on my right. The other man said something I didn't quite catch. I politely asked him to repeat it.

"I'm Charlie," he said, smiling broadly. He was holding a folder in his lap.

"I'm Jack," I said. "How can I help you?"

David, also smiling broadly, said, "We're here to look at wedding cakes."

"It's for our wedding," Charlie added.

I shifted uneasily in my seat, knowing instantly what my answer was to their request. What I wasn't sure of was how best to say it. Or how they would respond when I did.

"Sorry, guys," I said after a moment. "I don't do cakes for same-sex weddings."

For a moment, the two men just stared at me. They didn't say a word. As if they hadn't heard me or hadn't quite understood—or had heard and understood, but just couldn't believe I'd actually said what they'd just heard me say.

I chose my next words carefully.

"I'll sell you birthday cakes, shower cakes, cookies, or brownies. I just don't do cakes for same-sex weddings."

I explained that I didn't create cakes for same-sex weddings, that the two of them were welcome to anything else in my shop—birthday cakes, shower cakes, cookies, or brownies—but I couldn't prepare a wedding cake for them.

That brief exchange instantly tipped a long, long line of dominoes that have been falling ever since.

Charlie was still gripping the folder in front of him. I was to learn later that it contained their ideas for a custom wedding cake.

David suddenly leaped to his feet, yelling profanities that turned every head in the room. He flipped me off, spun on his heels, and stormed out of the nearest door, cursing all the way.

Charlie, still clenching his folder, stood up and turned without saying anything. He walked over to an older woman sitting at a nearby table. (She was his mother, it turned out.) She stood up too, and together they barged out the other door of the shop.

Nineteen words, approximately twenty seconds. That's all it took.

I was stunned.

I immediately realized that my answer wasn't necessarily the most complete or comprehensive one I could have offered, but their abrupt departure didn't allow for more explanation, or even any more conversation, which I would have preferred. Nevertheless, I felt that my answer was clear, honest, and to the point.

Still, I sat there, wondering if there was something else I could have said that would have expressed my intentions better before they stormed out. To this day, I don't know how I could have stated my thoughts more clearly. I only wish that we had been able to talk for a minute or two so I could have tried to explain to them that I gladly welcome and serve everyone, regardless of sexual orientation, race, religion, ethnicity, or gender identity. I really do serve everyone. Some cakes and designs I cannot create because of the content of the message that the imagery or words on the cake might convey, but I never make those decisions based on the identity of the person asking for the cake. On other occasions when I'd been asked to create something I could not in good conscience provide, I had at least been given the opportunity to talk it over with the customer, and we had always resolved the difference of opinion amicably.

That's right: this wasn't the first time I'd had to say no to a would-be customer's request. I've even turned down requests from people very close to me who've asked for designs I'm not willing to create. But that July afternoon was one of the few times I hadn't been able to talk through my reasons with the person asking and come to some kind of mutual understanding. Sad to say, it wouldn't be the last.

Fifteen or twenty minutes went by. Things settled down. Customers returned to their purchases, and my employees went back to their projects. I went back to my work in the kitchen. Then the phone rang.

I glanced up—both of the women working behind the counter still had their hands full. I motioned to them that I'd take care of the call as I reached for the phone.

"Masterpiece Cakeshop, this is Jack. Can I help you?"

"Yeah—you the guy that just refused to serve two gay men?"

That was quick.

"I'm not sure what you mean," I replied. I was scrambling, trying to discern where this was going. "I'd never refuse to serve anyone. Or to sell anything in my shop to anyone who—"

"But you did refuse to sell them a wedding cake, didn't you?"

I paused, then started over, measuring my words as carefully as the ingredients for one of my cakes.

"I sell anything in my shop to anyone. It's just that I can't create or design custom cakes that celebrate events—"

The caller interrupted with a slew of profanity. Then the phone went dead.

I was stunned. Again.

I'd probably have been a lot more stunned had I known that—almost a decade later—I'd still be saying these same words, in pretty much the same way, almost every day...trying to help people understand my decision.

Moments later, the phone rang again, and even though Lisa was free to answer it, I let her know I would take this call as well.

"Masterpiece Cakeshop, this is Jack. Can I help you?"

Profanity spewed from the phone. When the caller hung up, I let the women working with me know that I'd be answering the phone for the rest of the day. I took a few more angry, obscene calls before I closed up shop at 6:00 p.m. Even then, the phone kept ringing—I just stopped answering it, which was more than unusual for me. For almost twenty years, I had made it a point to try to answer every phone call or open the door to anyone, no matter what time it was.

O n the way home, I stopped by the grocery store to pick up a few things. Looking back, I was probably driving, parking, and walking on autopilot, my mind preoccupied with the events of the last few hours.

I walked through the double doors of the grocery store and froze. Everyone suddenly seemed to be staring at me. I felt the whole world closing in.

They hate me, I thought, imagining the dark thoughts behind all those glaring faces. *They all hate me*. Fear breathed a chill along the back of my neck. I wasn't sure what to do.

And then, just as suddenly, the words came to me…words the Apostle Paul wrote in 2 Timothy 1:7: "God has not given us a spirit of fear, but of power, and of love, and of a sound mind."

The "sound mind" part was the Lord's way of reassuring me, telling me that He was in control. I suddenly realized that I had no reason to fear. I looked around—no one was giving me a second glance, much less a cold stare. I was just another customer shopping for a few things for dinner. God was bigger than a few phone calls, than a lot of curse words, than two disappointed would-be customers.

I would continue to trust the only One worthy of my trust.

2

A Threat and an Opportunity

The day of my meeting with David and Charlie marked a new era for Masterpiece Cakeshop in more ways than one. For one thing, from that day to this, I became the primary person to answer the phone. I felt a responsibility to protect my employees from the horrific calls that began to flood our shop.

The phone was already ringing when I unlocked the shop door the next morning, and it kept ringing pretty much nonstop. I made myself wait to answer it—a first—until we opened for business at seven. From then on, the calls continued unabated until I stopped answering them again at 6:00 p.m. Virtually every call was hateful, profane, or threatening. I marveled at how quickly word of yesterday's incident had spread and at how many people were eager to verbally attack someone they'd never met or heard of before.

How angry (or hurting) do you have to be, I wondered, *to wake up with this kind of hate?* Think about it. The alarm goes off, you grab a shower, get the kids ready for school, take a sip of coffee, chew a bite of

toast—see an email, read a tweet—and see that a little cake shop out in
Colorado isn't creating cakes for same-sex weddings. And that tears it.

You're suddenly so angry that you can't do anything until you've
given that shop owner a piece of your mind. He's got it coming! In fact,
you're going to tell your friends to do the same: call him and let him have
an earful.

Or email him. By the time I woke up that day, a couple hundred
emails were already sitting in my inbox, and that number grew all day
long. And—again—almost every one was hateful. (I'd offer you a few
examples, but as a reporter later said while scrolling through them,
"Everything here is too vile to put on the [TV] screen.")

The next few days offered more of the same. Hour after hour after
hour. I began to really wonder how long this might go on.

After a few days of this, I answered another phone call, bracing myself
for yet another vitriolic earful.

"Masterpiece Cakeshop, this is Jack. Can I help you?"

"You the owner?"

"I am," I said, smiling into the receiver. I had made a conscious decision to be friendly and cheerful, no matter what came next. My faith in
Christ teaches me that everyone is valuable and loved by God, and I want
to treat them with love and respect.

"I'm in my car, and I'm heading to your shop." The voice was flat
but menacing in a way that made me stop what I was doing and listen
closely to what he said. "I've got a gun, and I'm coming to your store to
blow your head off." He hung up.

Was this for real, or just another crazy call? I'd had so many of the
latter those last few days. But Lisa was working in the back that morning,
and my four-year-old granddaughter was with her. I decided to err on
the side of caution.

"What's up, Dad?" Lisa's voice was apprehensive.

"I just got another call," I said. "But this one sounds as if it might
be dangerous." I paused, letting it sink in for both of us.

"Some guy says he's got a gun and he's on his way here. I want you to stay in the back and don't come out until I tell you it's safe. I'm gonna call the police."

Lisa took her little girl's hand and did as I asked. I dialed 911 and explained my situation to the dispatcher. She said she would send an officer right away.

The phone rang again. It was the same caller renewing his threat, telling me how close he was, even naming the streets. Then again: he said something that indicated to me that he knew my daughter was in the shop. And so the calls kept coming, every few seconds—each more menacing than the last—while I waited with one eye on the clock and one on the parking lot.

Finally, a police cruiser pulled up outside. The officer came to the door.

I thanked him for coming, then explained the situation, the conversation of a few days earlier, and all that had transpired after that. As we were talking, the phone rang—and caller ID confirmed it was the same man, once again. This time, the policeman answered, but the caller merely hung up. He continued doing that for a few minutes: call, hang up, call, hang up. He never stayed on the line long enough for the policeman to trace his number.

That made me wonder if he was just a crank, making empty threats. Or had he been serious but changed his mind when he saw the officer's car in our parking lot? I'll never know. But he certainly prompted me to rethink the seriousness of some of the other calls and emails I'd been getting. Soon, we'd be installing an alarm system and surveillance cameras—something my little cake shop had never needed before.

By God's grace, to my knowledge, I never heard from that particular caller again. And I wish I could say the threats of physical violence ended there too. But they've continued, off and on, through the years—including one man who made it a point, for quite a long while, to call me up at regular intervals to tell me I wasn't fit to live, that he owned a machete, and that one of these days he'd be coming in to chop me into little pieces. So far, he hasn't done that.

Even when talking to the guy with the machete, I have tried to keep a smile in my voice. I always hope that, if given the chance, I might be able to share God's love and grace with him. Yes, even him. Where else is he going to hear it? On TV? The internet? Read it in a newspaper? From his closest friends? Does he *have* any close friends? That man—like every one of the rest of us—needs to hear about God's grace and how Jesus came and died on a cross to pay the penalty for our sins and restore our broken relationship with the Father.

Actually, I have prayed for that opportunity with everyone who calls, and quite a few times, I have gotten that chance. Just two days after David and Charlie came through my shop, I took a call from a man who said he was an atheist from up in the Northwest. He wanted to talk about what had happened. He was polite, genuinely interested, and we talked for most of an hour. I explained exactly what had happened between the two men and myself, that I was happy to serve them and happy to sell them anything else in my shop, or to create other custom work for them. It was just the iconic nature of the wedding cake itself that was problematic. I also took the opportunity to share what I believe is the best news in the world: The Bible says we are separated from God the Father by our sin. It says clearly that Jesus Christ left His throne in Heaven and became a man. He lived a sinless life and took the punishment for our sin when He died on the cross. He was buried, and when He rose from the dead, He proved that He had power over both sin and death, as well as the authority to restore our relationship with the Father.

The atheist on the phone was kind enough to let me share many aspects of my faith in Christ with him, and I gave him room to explain some of his lack of faith to me. We ended the call on friendly terms, and for me, at least, it was something of a life-changing conversation.

Before the events of that week opened the door to so many visits with people of vastly different points of view, I'd always thought of sharing my faith as something God might give me a special opportunity to do once in a great while. After my phone call with the atheist, though, I suddenly realized that those kinds of opportunities were probably around me all the time, every day—I'd just never looked for them, much less taken advantage of them.

Starting that Saturday, I began looking. I always wanted to be alert, able, and willing to share Christ with anyone I met. What's the point of suddenly being on so many people's radars if you can't use those moments to share with them your deepest beliefs? That, for me, is the best news in the whole world: the love of Jesus Christ.

My opportunities, I soon learned, were about to begin in earnest.

3

Protests and Publicity

Not long after David and Charlie paid me their visit, I heard they'd be coming to see me again.

More specifically, they were coming as part of a protest that would take place in front of my shop. The protestors showed up on a Saturday, and even though they were few in number, they still drew some local media, who soon made the men's complaints more widely known. Those reporters announced another protest was scheduled for the following weekend.

This one, we were promised, would bring out a really big crowd.

One of the reporters covering one of the protests outside my shop made his way inside to fill me in on what was coming and to ask if I'd like to tell my side of the story.

I wasn't sure that was such a good idea and frankly told him so. I'd been interviewed on television only once before, many years earlier, when I demonstrated cake decorating live on a local news show. I didn't know much about microphones, and I tended to talk with my hands. Every time the producers cut to me to ask a few questions, I made some movement that produced a crackling sound on the mic they'd attached to my shirt. Nobody could understand a thing I said.

I had learned a good bit from that experience, but I also realized the subject was a little more serious this time around.

I didn't want to commit, but I also didn't want to back away. I tried to excuse myself. "I'm not sure..." I told the reporter. "If I say something stupid, I'm stuck with it."

He assured me that if I was unhappy with anything I said, he would let me redo it until I was satisfied. I believed him. We did the interview, and he was true to his word.

Later on, as my situation became a full-fledged court case working its way, step by step, up through the judicial system to the U.S. Supreme Court, I would take considerable care in crafting exactly what I did and didn't want to say. That day, though, I was still pretty much just speaking what was on my heart in the moment, and thankfully, God gave me—on the very first take—the words to say exactly what I wanted to communicate.

I told the reporter I was a follower of Jesus Christ, that I believe the biblical definition of a true marriage is the union of one man and one woman, and that I couldn't create or design a custom cake that celebrated any other concept of marriage.

I also assured him that I had nothing against the two men who disagreed with me, that they were welcome in my shop anytime, and that they were welcome to purchase anything available in my showcases. I added that I would even create other custom cakes for them—just not one that featured a message so contrary to my beliefs.

As I watched the interview when it aired that evening, I was satisfied that the reporter and his producers had sincerely tried to understand what I wanted to articulate. And even though they weren't able to play the entire conversation in such a short soundbite, I felt they did a good job of communicating my perspective.

A long with the phone calls and emails, I was now beginning to receive more visits from people in my shop who wanted to talk to me about my decision not to make the cake for David and Charlie. Some of them wanted to tell me how despicable I was; some of them wanted to commend my courage. Some of them wanted to debate my theology or just hear my reasoning from my own lips.

"You've been making my cakes for nearly twenty years," one woman told me. "But I'll never buy another one." I asked her why. "Because you're a bigot!" she said.

I asked her what made her think so. We wound up talking about our beliefs for a few minutes—but she's never been back to buy another cake.

Some of them tried to tell me the Bible endorses or allows for same-sex marriage. I gently expressed my disagreement...but told them I admired their boldness for coming in and talking with me face to face.

One guy who came through the door was a big, big man—220 pounds, tattoos everywhere, muscles everywhere—ex-military, Special Ops, he said. He told me of his service years ago in the Vietnam War. Then, with tears in his eyes, he told me I was one of the heroes of his life, pulled out a medal he'd received for his service, and gave it to me.

I've actually had several visits like that from veterans—some from Korea, some from Kuwait, some, like that man, from Vietnam. Somehow, they always seem a little larger than life, and they usually grow teary as we talk. And so do I.

A s I considered the approaching protest, I remembered that some people coming into the shop had told me of a social media post David and Charlie had made after they left my shop. The post, they said, had "gone viral." That could mean that thousands of people from every state and all over the world were rallying to their cause. If so, I had no idea what to expect from the coming protest.

The following week, true to their word, David and Charlie appeared with their "thousands" of fellow protestors. Actually, only about eighteen or twenty people showed up; I'm not sure of the exact number.

The media showed up though: all of Denver's top TV stations, the *Denver Post*, and a large independent newspaper were all on hand. Watching the news that night, you'd have thought from the camera angles that there were quite a few more lined up to oppose us—shouting, waving rainbow flags, holding up signs with phrases like "Let them eat cake." It was an important lesson in how those who control the media could greatly impact perceptions of my character, my beliefs, and—soon—my legal case.

When reporters interviewed me that day, I discovered for the first time that Colorado had passed a state law that called decisions like mine (declining to artistically express a particular message) an act of "discrimination."

I was stunned. Yet again.

I didn't discriminate against anyone! Those two guys were welcome in my shop, welcome to my cakes, welcome to anything short of my conscience. Surely the Constitution protected my conscience. If religious freedom didn't mean the right to live out my faith, what could it possibly mean?

I was simply exercising what I thought to be my constitutionally protected right to decline to design and create an artistic expression that violated my deeply held religious beliefs. Could the state actually be thinking of prosecuting me for something like this?

Was that what I had to look forward to?

How do you prepare to fight something like that?

4

Growing Up

In some ways, actually, I'd already been preparing. In some ways, I'd been preparing my whole life.

When I think about the neighborhood I grew up in and compare it to some of the stories I hear from friends about where and how they grew up, I realize that my home—Lakewood, Colorado—was really kind of a storybook place. All through my growing-up years, it offered wide alfalfa fields and the towering beauty of the nearby Rocky Mountains, perfect for mischief and adventure, running and roaming, building forts and treehouses. (One treehouse I built lasted long enough for me to show my own kids.)

We moved there in 1962, when I had just turned six, and Lakewood itself was just a neighborhood still seven years away from becoming an official town. Mine was the third family on our block; a fourth house was still being built, and the rest of the area was completely open and undeveloped. Cows grazed in nearby pastures, and pheasants sometimes flew up unexpectedly as we roamed through the fields, and meadowlarks sang their beautiful, distinctive songs. My best friend, Neil, lived just two doors down in the house with the only swing set on our street.

Soon the other houses filled in, lots of other kids my age crowded the neighborhood, and summer evenings meant long, happy games of hide-and-seek and Capture the Flag. Summer days meant baseball, basketball, riding unicycles—even playing basketball while riding unicycles. It was just a great time and a wonderful place to be a boy. Life was mostly good, and we were all mostly happy.

I attended a newly built school, Lasley Elementary. I was still a very young boy when they sent us home early one cool, clear November afternoon. I remember wondering what could be so important for them to cancel school…and then learning that President John F. Kennedy had been assassinated. That may have been my first wake-up call to the fact that the world was bigger than Lakewood—that not everything revolved around my family and friends, our neighborhood, and our problems.

It was also at Lasley that one of my favorite instructors informed my mom and dad during a parent-teacher conference that I had "constipation of the brain and diarrhea of the mouth." Maybe I was trying too hard to capture her attention—or maybe I was just a brat. Either way, it should have been my first inkling that not everyone might appreciate everything I had to say.

Junior high brought its own life lessons. Each morning, about a dozen of us stood on the corner across the street from my house and waited for the school bus. Since ours was only the second stop on the route, we competed aggressively to see who could board first and grab one of those coveted back seats.

One day, a slightly older boy from the neighborhood—one for whom I'd already been developing a growing respect—stepped forward and extended his arm to prevent us boys from getting on and, incredibly, let the girls get on first. I was genuinely shocked that someone would put others ahead of himself like that.

I had never even thought of doing that. In fact, even though I joined the others in teasing him about it, that was probably the first time I'd seen such an unexpected and unrequired act of selflessness demonstrated in real life. With that one singular, outstanding move, that young man won a whole new level of my respect. I thought, *He'll be president some-day.* (He's not—yet—but he is a lawyer with a great reputation among his peers.)

As years went by, and after I became a Christian, I thought of what that friend did... of the fact that he stood alone for what he thought was right... of other unselfish acts I'd seen from Christians and non-Christians alike... and it made me want to follow their example. If people who didn't believe in Jesus could be so courageously selfless, didn't I have an even greater responsibility to be that brave, standing for His love and truth with those I came in contact with each day?

After all, if I was watching, other people were watching. And I wanted them to see Christ in me.

I had been eagerly anticipating my junior high science classes—dissecting frogs, mixing chemicals in actual test tubes and beakers. What I had not anticipated was my lab partner. He intimidated me, and I was at least a little bit afraid of him. He would do things like pour the alcohol out of our lamp onto the table and then set it on fire. It caused quite a commotion, but looking back, I assume that was mostly an annoyance, since our teacher had merely sent us out to sit in the hall, rather than having us expelled. I spent a fair amount of seventh grade science class out in the hall missing experiments, and that turned into poor test scores and the first bad grades of my academic career.

Whatever her reasons for punishing me along with my lab partner (maybe that whole "constipation of the brain" thing came back), that science teacher taught me a couple of unscientific things that have come back to me often in recent years. One, that those in authority don't always care that you didn't do anything wrong. And two, how quickly you can be sidelined if you're labeled a "troublemaker."

But if junior high was my first real experience with unjust punish-ment, it was also my first real introduction to something that would change my life forever: art.

When I say "introduction," I don't mean that I hadn't enjoyed art classes before. Even in elementary school, I liked listening to Miss Nelson talk about classic paintings like *American Gothic* and *Pinkie* and *The Blue Boy*, tremendous painters like Grant Wood and Rembrandt, or the basics of blending colors and something called "impressionistic" art. For me, art class was as wonderful as recess. There just was nothing like it.

In junior high, I was introduced to the concept of electives and the freedom to choose for myself certain select classes on different subjects. Not just math or science classes either, but options like music (choir, ensembles, or band), foreign languages (Spanish, French)...and the one that instantly caught my eye: art.

I just couldn't believe my school would give me graduation credit for drawing and painting. And even for trying new things, like sculpting and other unexplored media.

Each semester, I would look over the list of art electives and try to check off something new. Mr. McBride was the main art teacher at my school. He was a fun, enthusiastic teacher and a gifted artist who was genuinely invested in his students and had a way of stirring their interest in his subject. Watching him in class, I began to realize that you could actually make a career out of being an artist—a satisfying career too, and one that paid the bills. (I was beginning to understand that everything isn't always just given to you.)

High school offered even better opportunities for a budding artist: more equipment and two gifted art teachers who really seemed to want to encourage and nurture their students' talents.

Mr. Filson headed up the drawing and painting classes, while Mr. Glasgow handled pottery and sculpting. Some semesters, I was able to take two classes a day in the art rooms, one from each of them.

In the drawing rooms, we often worked from still-life settings: old milk jugs, horse collars, umbrellas, blankets. The goal was not only to draw what was in front of us, but to learn how to do that using a variety of different styles, from line drawings (working to show as much detail or texture as possible) to thirty-second speed sketches where the objective was to draw as much as possible as quickly as possible. Sometimes we focused on contrasts, showing anything we saw in any sort of shadow as completely black—no shades of gray whatsoever—while leaving the rest of the page absolutely white.

But my favorite projects in Mr. Filson's class involved students, as part of the setting, taking turns modeling for their peers' sketches. I loved to draw people and was just as pleased when it was my turn to be the model. Mr. Filson posed me in a suede leather jacket that had fringe on the sleeves. This was probably one of the lessons where we practiced detail drawing, and, knowing how frustrating it was for the artists when their model moved, I foolishly declined to take a break, even when Mr. Filson offered me one. I wanted my classmates to have as much time as possible to get their detailed work done without having to deal with a suddenly rearranged fringe.

But as I sat, cross-legged, immobile, I gradually felt my legs go to sleep and finally become completely numb. Still, I didn't move—maintaining my pose for nearly an hour until Mr. Filson dismissed the class. Relieved, I finally hopped off the table where I'd heroically held my pose, only to crumple to the floor in a heap. It took a little while to get the blood flowing in my legs again, and I was probably late for my next class, but it made for another memorable day in the art rooms . . . and helped me to further understand (even though I wasn't yet a Christian) what it means to put other people before myself, even when it wasn't easy.

One afternoon during some free time, I came into the pottery room to find Mr. Glasgow, the pottery teacher, painting with watercolors. I watched in amazement as he gently applied layer after layer, creating an incredibly beautiful landscape. He asked if I wanted to try my hand at it, and I jumped at the chance. He explained the different types of paper available, and how each interacted with the paints, making it clear which paper was his favorite (and it became mine as well). He also showed me how to use different kinds of brushes and techniques to bring my paintings to life. While I've never attained his level of quality in my own watercolor work, the skills Mr. Glasgow taught me are techniques that I use daily in creating artistic cakes.

I think often of those two teachers and how God placed them in my high school at just the right time and used them in just the right ways to equip me with skills I would need later on.

Ironically, it was the lack of help I received from another high school teacher—or rather, counselor—that led me to the most fulfilling career I could have imagined.

Like all seniors, I was required to sit down with a career counselor to discuss my future vocational goals. I say required, because it is not something that I ever would have done voluntarily. Unfortunately, this meeting didn't take place until the spring, so there was no time to make any adjustments to my electives.

I remember sitting across the desk from a man who seemed to have as little interest in our meeting as I did. He asked what kind of ambitions I was nurturing and what kind of career I hoped to pursue.

"I'd like to be an architect," I said, probably with some enthusiasm, as I had always loved to design buildings and floorplans, and it seemed to me to be a perfect career choice. His response surprised me.

"You don't have enough math," he said without looking up, his eyes scanning my transcripts.

That would have been helpful to know a few years ago, I thought, *when I was choosing my electives.* Not that I would have skipped any of those art classes; I just might have made some different math and science choices. *So now what?* I wondered.

He asked what a second option might be.

"I'd like to be an artist."

"There's no money in art," he said. Period. No emotion, no suggestions for how I might still get on track with either of those dreams. Simply silence and a blank stare.

My future, apparently, looked dim. Both of us could see me winding up as a common laborer of some kind—doing something I wasn't equipped for, wasn't enthused about, and that probably didn't pay much. I left his office thinking, *I should have planned better.*

Still, when I graduated a few weeks later in the spring of 1974, I had a job. I'd been working since my junior year at a local pizza parlor, making the pizzas and washing the dishes. The work wasn't bad, just not very interesting or challenging. The guys I worked with were entertaining enough, but I didn't like working Friday and Saturday nights and coming home smelling like cheese. Moving out into "the real world," I was hoping for something that paid more and smelled better.

5

Learning

I don't know why I hadn't really considered working at the Golden Cream Donut Company, a large wholesale bakery (a factory really) that produced hundreds of cakes every week and thousands of donuts, cinnamon rolls, pies, and cakes every day. The owner, Mr. Lee (Charlie, as he was affectionately known), was a neighbor of ours who had previously employed most of my family. It should have been a natural choice for me to take my turn.

Immediately after graduation, I applied, was hired, and showed up precisely at 10:00 a.m. on Thursday, June 6, 1974, ready for work and whatever came next.

What came next was all new to me, but soon I grew acclimated to the actual working environment. Work here and do this for two hours, take a ten-minute break in there, return here, do it again for two more hours. Take thirty minutes for lunch—no more, no less—then return here, repeat your previous tasks for two more hours, take another ten-minute break, put in two more hours, clock out, then come back tomorrow and do it again.

It took a little while to adjust to a real workaday job and working with people who were not my age. These people had been working for years—some of them for decades—in this industry, packing donuts into boxes, keeping production numbers high, readying our products for on-time deliveries, keeping the worksite clean and sanitary. If you kept up, you fit in and could join in the cheerful atmosphere; if you didn't, you felt isolated in a hurry. For me, it was a whole new world.

My first regular assignment was on a wrapping detail. Besides selling thousands of items that were delivered all across the Denver area and running a busy retail store up front, Golden Cream also sold prepackaged pastries suitable for vending machines, convenience stores, and other outlets. My first assignment was in the department that handled the packaging—or rather handled the great and complicated machine that handled the packaging.

Ideally, this machine, fed from a roll of cellophane on top, took the fresh pastries entering on its left side, neatly wrapped them, and sent them out its right side. When that happened, it was my job to help sort the emerging packages into baskets, then line the baskets up so delivery drivers could load them and deliver them to their final destinations.

I say "ideally," because the machine didn't always work as neatly as the engineers who designed it intended. Quite often, the packages would come out sealed in the middle, rather than on the ends. When that happened, the man in charge of the department would start to swear…at the machine, at his coworkers, at no one in particular. He swore loudly and colorfully while hurling the defective packages at the wall or the floor. He threw some magnificent tantrums, and I was amazed that nobody ever called him out for it.

I wondered if this type of behavior was actually acceptable in this new world. Even to my teenage my mind, his fits seemed immature and disrespectful of his coworkers, his employer—even himself. They also stood in stark contrast to the basic principles of good behavior I'd learned in school, in church, even at the back of the school bus.

Fortunately, I only had to put up with all of that for a few weeks. I was soon reassigned to a more permanent position as a "roll icer." My new duties were simple enough. I first removed the baked products—pecan rolls, bow ties, cherry cheese danishes, or cinnamon twists (I loved those)—from the sheet pans, then lined them up and fed them through another machine, which spread a delicious icing on their tops. I was responsible for controlling the amount of icing each item received and doing so as quickly and efficiently as possible. It sounds simple, and it was.

So I gave myself a challenge. I decided to take what seemed to me to be one of the lowliest positions in the whole bakery and use it to my advantage. I was going to be the best roll icer ever. I made up my mind that no one would be as fast as me or put the icing on as proficiently as I did. With racks and racks of rolls to ice each day, I had plenty of opportunities to practice.

The biggest drawback to all of this was not the amount of work; everyone in the shop had a lot to do. My biggest problem was the texture of the cinnamon twists. When sugar, cinnamon, oil, water, and some secret ingredients were all baked together, they formed a very abrasive surface (much like picking up sandpaper all day), which, by the end of each work week (Thursday afternoon) had worn the skin right off my fingertips, making them exceedingly sensitive. So sensitive that I couldn't touch too many things without feeling a sting. The weekends gradually brought healing and relief, but I probably complained to more people than I should have.

Fourteen long, grueling months after I started, a job appeared on the bulletin board for a baking/mixing job in the Pie Department. The job included a pay increase. My chances of securing it were slim, as I had very little seniority, and we were a union shop—meaning the person with the highest seniority would be awarded the job, regardless of their qualifications. Still, I applied and waited, and, in the end, mine was the only name on the list.

I wondered why. Perhaps it was because of the schedule: I was required to begin work for this position at 4:00 a.m. (a time when, at that stage of my life, I was more likely to be going to bed than getting up). Or it could have been the foreman: a man named Eddie, about whom I'd already heard stories. Eddie had a reputation as a hardworking man, rarely taking breaks and expecting exceptional work—not only from himself, but from everyone under his command.

Perfection was a tall order for a young man who had never done this kind of work before (it still eludes me, even today). And believe me, I made plenty of mistakes. At times, I was sure I was ruining more products than I sent out. You wouldn't believe how many ways there are to mess up a batch of cake batter, or buttercreme, or coconut cream pie filling, or really any of the thirty or forty different products I was personally responsible for creating each day. Each product had multiple ingredients that needed to be handled in a multitude of specific ways, and I learned to take into account many things: product temperatures and mixing times, weights, volumes, etc. Baking is an art. Or a science. Or something else that takes a great deal of time and energy and care to learn. I was willing to put in the time and energy, but were Eddie and the management at Golden Cream willing to pay for my "education"?

I'm sure they had their doubts along the way. There's no telling how many mornings my phone rang at five minutes after four o'clock with Eddie on the line asking, "You comin' in this morning?"

Fortunately, both Golden Cream and Eddie were patient with me. Gradually, I learned the things that make for a dependable and profitable employee, and I really came to love my job, which I considered the best in the company. Most people at Golden Cream could only say, "I work in a bakery." I could say, "I am a baker."

But the best was yet to come.

A few years after I arrived at Golden Cream, Mr. Lee bought out another local bakery and brought its workers into our facility. Some of those employees were specialists at making something Golden Cream hadn't offered: custom cakes.

I had never seen anything like this before. As I said, our shop was more of a production plant that processed thousands of items every day. This new department made one cake at a time. One custom cake at a time. Artistic cakes, created using techniques that I had never seen... but similar to things I'd learned in my art classes at school.

The decorators' arrival sealed an idea that had been slowly forming in my head over the previous year or two—the notion of one day owning my very own bakery. Suddenly, I knew how I would do it. I knew how it would look. I would open a bakery devoted to designing custom cakes. Though I had no business training or formal business plan, I was sure my idea would succeed. I even knew what the name of my bakery would be: Masterpiece Cakeshop. "Masterpiece" said "art," while "Cakeshop" said "cakes." You wouldn't enter the shop looking for a loaf of bread, a donut, or a pie.

I wanted it to be a place where I could combine my gifts, talents, and art training with my love and knowledge of baking to create and design beautiful, artistic custom cakes.

I also knew it would take money. A great deal of money. In the meantime, I was going to focus on enjoying my current job and becoming the best baker I could be. I even grew to love and respect Eddie. He took the time to help me learn from my mistakes and understand the principles involved in successful baking. What's more, his patience with me taught me a great deal about working with many different kinds of people and personalities.

And he never threw any tantrums.

Along with the money and the desire to open my own place, I needed one more thing—something I had never really factored in.

Or more precisely, someone.

6

My Dream Girl

One October evening in 1975, I clocked out after my normal 10:00 a.m. to 6:30 p.m. shift and, as usual, headed for home. I wanted to clean up and grab a bite to eat before hitting the streets of Lakewood in my bright orange MG sports car to join friends for whatever adventure the evening air had to offer.

That particular night, I headed to Taco Bell to grab something for dinner. What caught my eye, though, as I walked through the door was not on the menu, but totally captivated me from the moment I stepped into the restaurant. A beautiful girl with dark brown hair and big blue eyes greeted me with, "How can I help you?"

I was stunned. (Pleasantly, for a change.) This girl even made the company-issued polyester brown uniform look...well, stunning.

She looked at me expectantly.

I stuttered out my order, and while I was waiting for the food, we talked. Her name was Debi. Our conversation went well enough that I asked when her shift ended, and then if it would be okay to meet her after work. She said yes.

It was late, probably somewhere around midnight, when I again met the girl I'd been thinking about all evening while hanging out with my friends. Apparently, I did more than just think about her; I must have done a fair amount of talking too, because she later told me some of my buddies had gone to Taco Bell asking if "Debi" was there. She inquired why they were asking, and soon understood why they wanted to know. They had figured out I was in love.

Fortunately, so was she.

An unexpected problem popped up the next time I showed up at Taco Bell to see this girl again...she wasn't there. I decided I must have misunderstood her schedule. The next day, I was back and still no Debi. I returned again and again over the next week. No Debi.

I ate breakfast, lunch, and dinner (and midnight snacks) at Taco Bell, hoping to find her again. (I knew I should have gotten a phone number.)

This was crazy. What could have happened to her?

I could have asked the other people working there what had happened to her, but that would have been too easy. No, I needed to be successful on this hunt myself. No assistance. I had to find this girl.

As it turned out, a medical condition kept her away from work for almost two weeks. But as soon as she returned, we reconnected, and I asked her out on our first "official" date. Again, she said yes.

This time, though, it was my turn to disappear (and disappoint). That was the week I was awarded the baking job in Eddie's department. My new 4:00 a.m. schedule was set to begin the very next day, and I was afraid that if I overslept, showed up late, or anything else, they might take away the job as easily as they'd given it.

I had to decide: Debi or my job? Since Debi and I hadn't even been on an official date, I foolishly chose the job.

That could have been the end of it, but Debi surprised me by deciding to stay in my corner and wait for me.

We did go out on our first date that weekend, and it was great. Things went well, and it looked like we might have a future.

A short time after we actually started dating, though, we broke up. The breakup didn't last too long, and we consequently dated again, broke up, dated again, and broke up again quite a few times in our early days.

The only real reason we ended up staying together was because one day, early in our relationship—at a time when I still had no relationship with God whatsoever—I sensed Him telling me that He had chosen Debi specifically for me. My response to this "revelation" was, "Really? Debi?" Followed by, "Okay...if You say so." (It's funny that without even knowing Him, I was trusting Him in this very important decision.)

And so in my heart, I made a commitment to pursue Debi.

It took quite a while, but on Friday, August 25, 1978, we were married in the courthouse in Golden, Colorado, witnessed by a good friend from Golden Cream and his wife. A simple reception followed at our home on Sunday. Only close family members were there, and I believe my grandma purchased our wedding cake—a simple, traditionally designed two-tiered cake from a local grocery store.

We've been married for over forty years now, with quite a few ups and downs. Every day of those years has affirmed that God chose this woman just for me—her strengths balanced my weaknesses, and her straight-and-narrow discipline and ability to organize and execute plans were perfect to balance my sometimes haphazard approaches. She focused my often-wandering attention. She knew how to help me keep my priorities straight and how to help me evaluate my less-thought-through decisions in constructive ways.

While I'm doing all the fun aspects of the job—making the cakes, meeting the customers—she takes care of the details, the numbers, the drier tasks that have to be done responsibly. Masterpiece Cakeshop would not be in business without her.

She's also more disciplined in her faith than almost anyone I've ever known, and her trust in the Lord and her daily walk with God are an inspiration to me, as is her influence on her family and friends. I constantly marvel that God understood so clearly exactly what I would need in a helpmate[1] and loved me enough to keep pointing me in the direction of that great heart and those beautiful eyes.

Together, we have raised a family, started and maintained a business for nearly thirty years, and weathered the persecutions and challenges this book describes. Our lives have been wonderfully full and good and incredibly better for living them together.

7

Meeting God

Sometime during the spring of 1979, maybe a Wednesday or Thursday, probably in March, I had finished my shift at Golden Cream—a twelve-hour overtime shift that started at 10:00 p.m.—and headed home.

That's when the most important event of my life happened.

Some backstory first.

While growing up in Lakewood, attending school, playing with my friends, and doing so many normal things, another normal part of my life was church attendance. My family went to Sunday school and church every week. And each week we sang songs, heard sermons, and were taught Bible lessons. I learned about David and Goliath, Daniel and the lions' den, Moses, Joseph and Mary, and a host of other characters. I was taught about important Middle Eastern places; some were familiar, but others had strange and unpronounceable names: Antioch, Beersheba, Caesarea, Laodicea, Israel, Eden, Moab, Rome...Most of this period was a blur. It was information I knew I would never need to remember for very long and didn't care much about. I did enjoy going to church each week to be with friends, but the "church" part never had much of a grip on me or my heart.

I quit attending when I was about seventeen, and by the time I was working full-time at Golden Cream, my shifts always included Sundays. Even if I had wanted to go to church (which I didn't), my day was already planned, so any thought about church or religion quickly faded into the rearview.

Debi's family was nominally Catholic, and while they had attended mass at Christmas, Easter, and occasionally some other services, it wasn't a strictly followed faith or one that had much of an impact on her life or her decisions. Sundays, to her, were also pretty much like any other day.

As I headed to my car that spring morning, one of the guys from my department asked if I wanted to go across the street with him to the Sandbar for a beer before I headed home. It was common practice to go over for a drink or two, and maybe an early morning "dinner" after work; a few of the guys from the night crew were probably already there.

I begged off, telling him I would see him the next day. I hopped into my old blue '66 Mustang and headed off toward Wheat Ridge, a suburb just northwest of Denver, where Debi and I rented a small apartment. She would be there waiting for me with our two little ones, Jeremy and Jennifer (Lisa hadn't been born yet).

Normally, when I got home, I would park the car, head into our home, and after catching up briefly, would head directly to bed. The kids were young enough that it was probably time for their morning naps, and it would have been a quiet house.

As I was heading north on Kipling, just about a mile or two from home, suddenly, without warning or invitation, I was stunned by a presence in my car. No, I was actually stunned by a *Person* in my car, not just a presence. I hesitate to say this because I know how it sounds, but the "Person" in my car that morning was God, or more precisely, the Holy Spirit. (I have always thought that if I had the presence of mind to look to the passenger seat on my right, I would be able to describe Him, maybe even paint or draw a picture of Him!) From here on, though, for the benefit of the reader, I'll simply call Him "God"...you can decide how you want to interpret it.

As it was, I did not have the presence of mind to even glance in His direction. Something incredible was happening. This interaction was not just unusual, it wasn't just important—it was a life-changing and eternity-altering encounter. Since I didn't feel that I had a choice about whether this would continue, I gave it my entire attention.

When God speaks, you pay attention. Complete attention. I was listening and listening intently.

My mind flashed back to lessons I had heard in my Sunday school days where sometimes people in the Bible, when confronted with mere angels, fell down on their faces "as if dead." I thought of Daniel, the Old Testament prophet, being terrified and falling prostrate at the feet of Gabriel,[1] or the Apostle Paul, who fell to the ground in the presence of Jesus after being blinded and asked, "Who are You, LORD?"[2] Then there was Mary, who after hearing God's wonderful message, proclaimed, "Behold, the bondslave of the Lord; may it be done to me according to Your word," and immediately broke into song, singing, "My soul exalts the Lord, and my spirit has rejoiced in God my Savior."[3]

There are many ways to respond to an encounter like this: fear, panic, terror, or even joy.

As these accounts rolled through my mind in the presence of the Person in my car, I continued to drive, uncertain but feeling no fear. I knew exactly Who was talking to me. In fact, throughout the exchange, I felt a kind of calm peace—even though I knew in my bones that the GOD of the UNIVERSE was confronting me with the inevitability of my very dark future without Him. He was letting me know that this very dark future could change right there and then.

God had come to rescue me.

Incredibly, though, His first action was to convict me of my sin!

I say "sin," rather than "sins," because my "sins" weren't the problem. They were the evidence of my problem. My "sin" was the real problem.

To discuss it as "sins" would be to say, for example, that when I lied last Tuesday, that made me a liar, and I could make some restitution to whomever I had lied. Or when I stole something on Thursday, that made me a thief, and again, I could make restitution to somebody. The problem was, I lied on Tuesday because I am a liar. I stole because I already am a thief. I sinned because I was a sinner! Not the other way around. The fact that I was a sinner in the core of my being was the problem that needed to be dealt with.

My sin was an affront to God. It sprang from and demonstrated my rebellion against Him and His law.

If I sin against you, you can choose to forgive me or not. It's up to you. If you choose not to, you would be the one bearing the consequences of maybe having an unforgiving heart. That's about it. No eternal consequences.

When we sin against God, though, it becomes a much deeper problem, and even if it seems logical that He could simply forgive us, that is a problem for a couple of reasons. The Bible says in Proverbs 17:15, "Acquitting the guilty and condemning the innocent—the Lord detests them both." Think about that and I think that you'd agree: He can't simply "acquit the guilty." That would be detestable to Him. Simply forgiving is also problematic because the "wages of sin is death," according to the book of Romans.[4] Sin must be punished. By simply forgiving without some form of punishment or payment, God would be doing something that He Himself detests! Sin must be paid for. And it has to be punished.

But God, being rich in mercy, because of His great love for us, so that He might show the immeasurable riches of His grace for us,[5] sent His only begotten Son, that whoever believes on Him should not perish, but have everlasting life.[6]

Christ Jesus came into the world to save sinners....[7] For God did not send His Son into the world to condemn the world, but to save the world through Him.[8] And, who can forgive sins, but God alone?[9]

I was a sinner, and He came to rescue me.

All of this—the Scripture, the biblical characters, my own rebellion—was unfolding as I drove down Kipling, and it all happened in less than a few seconds.

My first response was admission. "You're right, God, I am a sinner." I knew I needed a Savior, and that Savior could only be Jesus Christ. Salvation is only available through Him because of His sinless life as the God who humbled Himself and became a man.[10] He lived a life complete with all the temptations I would later experience, yet He did it without sinning.[11] His death on the cross was punishment for sin. My sin. All sin. His resurrection from the dead was proof of His innocence, and it showed His absolute authority over death, sin, and the grave.

Jesus said, "You must be born again."[12] He was giving me the opportunity to experience His love and forgiveness right there and then.

I finally began to understand the most important lesson that I had ever heard in church or Sunday school.

Jesus came to give life. Jesus came to give life abundantly. He came to give me life.

That was really good news!

My response, though, was to try to negotiate. Looking back, this was probably one of the most foolhardy acts of my entire life.

The God of Creation was calling me. Beckoning me. He was letting me know that He had created me to have a relationship with Him. A good relationship. One that was more beautiful and glorious than anything I could ever imagine. He wasn't just "saving" me from Hell. He wasn't even exiling me to "Heaven," where I'd imagined I'd be bored to tears for eternity.

No, He was rescuing me from death and slavery to sin to LIFE and FREEDOM IN HIM! Not simply existing, but being ALIVE and FREE![13] This would be a life lived in an intimate relationship with Someone Who absolutely loved me. Someone Who created me with a purpose, compared to the shallow life I was pursuing on my own. I felt as though I was really beginning to get it.

Yet there I was, getting ready to bargain with God, to negotiate.

My "negotiation" was short-lived, and it went like this:

"Let me clean up my life and You'll get a better deal."

"You can't."

Period. That was His reply. I realized in that instant that there was absolutely nothing I needed to do—or even that I *could* do—to complete what God had already accomplished through the work of Jesus Christ on the cross. No work. No good deed. No repayment. Nothing. Anything that I would do or try to do to enhance, improve, or add to His work on the cross would not only tarnish the beauty and value of His sacrifice, but would erase its purpose.

I couldn't do a thing—and that was the point. "For it is by GRACE you are saved, through FAITH...not by works..." I had nothing to add to the equation. His sacrifice covered everything.[14]

I understood.

"You're right. I'm Yours."

It was set. It was final. I surrendered.

Two minutes earlier, my life had been mine. But my life was empty. Now, I had no idea what life would bring, but I knew Who was going to bring it. I would trust Him.

Suddenly, though, a new and unexpected problem popped into my mind.

In a few moments, I would come face to face with Debi. How would I tell her? It's hard enough to explain this salvation thing when I can sit down and write it out, after giving everything a great deal of thought and contemplation. Right then, though, I was heading to our apartment, and I needed to be prepared. Completely prepared.

I wasn't.

I think I probably parked the car in the garage, walked into our kitchen, and gave Debi a brief "hello," followed by something like, "How's everything? How are the kids?" It would have been simple and innocuous, something that wouldn't lead to further conversation. She responded with something equally innocent, and I followed with, "Goodnight, I'm going to bed. See you in a bit."

"Going to bed" for me normally meant slipping under the covers, laying my head on the pillow, closing my eyes, and falling sound asleep within seconds—something that still holds true today.

That morning, however, sleep eluded me. I tossed and turned. I rearranged the covers. I made sure the curtains were pulled tight. Still, I could not fall asleep. God was telling me to get up, get out of bed, and to go tell Debi about the transformation that had just taken place in my heart, in my life, in my soul. That was something I wasn't prepared to do, at least not just yet. Maybe after a good sleep...maybe.

Telling Debi what had happened was really kind of scary. No, it was *terrifying*—and not something I wanted to do. You see, just a few weeks before, my sister-in-law Teresa had invited Debi to go to church with her, and Debi had uncharacteristically exploded about how Christians are hypocrites. When Debi related the conversation to me, it was with such passion that I thought, *Poor Teresa will probably never ask her to church again. In fact, Teresa will probably never ask anyone to church again—ever!*

I figured that I at least should face that kind of confrontation only after a good sleep.

But sleep continued to elude me. I tried everything I could think of. Nothing helped.

For the second time that morning, I decided to try to negotiate with God.

"God, when I tell her, there's a good possibility that she'll leave me, but You know that."

"Tell her."

"She might take it better later, after I can think of a good way to phrase it."

"I want you to get up and tell her now."

"I'm sure she'll leave, and it would be easier to handle if I do it on a full night's sleep."

"Tell her now. I'll be with you. Trust Me."

The negotiation ended right there, and I got out of bed and headed for the kitchen.

Debi was as surprised to see me out of bed as I was to be out of bed.

She looked at me without saying a word, but her eyes questioned me. *Why are you up? You should be asleep. What's going on? What's wrong?*

Still hoping for a reprieve, I hesitated. None came, so I stammered, then said kind of bluntly, "I...I became a Christian today."

Her delay in replying made me wonder. *What is she thinking? How will she answer?*

The few moments it took for Debi to reply seemed like forever, but when she did, her answer stunned me.

"Me too. Three days ago. Now we have something in common."

I don't remember the rest of the conversation, except that when she had told me about my sister-in-law's invitation to church, apparently, I'd gently suggested she might reconsider, if only out of courtesy. Incredibly, Debi had actually heeded that suggestion, gone to church, and heard the Gospel that morning, probably for the very first time in her life. A few days later, while vacuuming the floor of our house, she found herself having a conversation very like the one I'd had in the car that morning with that same unseen Person I had sensed. And, like me, she'd simply, quietly realized the depths of her sinful nature and her need for a Savior. She, too, had given her life to Christ.

Her conversion was as unexpected and powerful as mine. We had both been saved, rescued, redeemed, born again in the same week, by the same God, after realizing the same truth: That we were both sinners in our core beings. Sinners who not only needed to be rescued from an eternity away from God, but sinners whose punishment and separation had been paid for by that same God. There was nothing to add, nothing to do to enrich or enhance His love for us. We were sinners who were now able to participate in this wonderful relationship with Him and who now, from that very moment, were embarking on a new life. A new way to live, a new way to work, a new way to raise our kids, a new way to approach our marriage, handle our money, everything! I sure was glad that I got out of bed and told Debi my great news![15]

It was the most amazing day of my life. I still look back and wonder.

When I do, I begin to realize how many things He had orchestrated in my life to bring me to that point and into this amazing relationship.

I remembered the art classes, the science classes, the school bus rides, the pizza parlors, all my friends, and the various experiences God led me through to bring me to that day. I thought about the night I went into Taco Bell, hungry for a simple Bell Beefer, and came out in love with the girl who would change my life, be my partner, and help guide our decisions and raise our kids. What a good and gracious gift from a good and gracious Father!

I knew that, as the book of Ephesians says, my future had been planned out for me from long ago.[16]

Years later I looked back again and realized that not only had I made a career in art, but I was also able to pay other people to use their artistic skills to do it as well, and I was able to use my architectural gifts to design three bakeries! Then I remembered how God used someone to direct me to the job that led to all those things.

To this day, I thank Him for bringing a high school counselor into my life to tell me that I had no future.

One of us was in the wrong job, but it wasn't me. Thank God!

8

Gaining Experience, Gaining Wisdom

Our family was growing. We soon had three children: Jeremy, Jennifer, and Lisa. And sometime late in 1978, Debi and I made the decision for her to leave her part-time job as a waitress in a high-class coffee shop so she could stay home and raise our kids. It was a tough call: she really loved her job, and we both understood it would be quite a stretch to cover all the expenses of raising a family on my income alone. And although Golden Cream Donut Company, and later King Soopers and Child's Pastry Garden, all paid very well (especially considering that I had no college education or formal training of any kind), we were trusting the Bible's promise that God would provide.[1]

God had given us these children to care for, and we felt a distinct responsibility to raise them in "the discipline and instruction of the Lord."[2] We were also convinced that no one loved our kids as much as we did, or ultimately had so much of their best interests at heart—not only their physical interests, but also their spiritual health and well-being.[3]

With our newfound faith came a deep desire to attend a Bible-believing church where we would learn about God and grow spiritually by hearing thoughtful teaching of His Word. We found such a church close to our home and began attending regularly. And I mean regularly: if my shift ended on Sunday morning at 10:30, and church started at 10:00, I'd be there—maybe a little bit late, but sitting in the very back row in white bakery jeans and a white bakery shirt, unconcerned about chocolate or raspberry stains, anxious to hear and learn more about this amazing God who loves us so much. I didn't want to miss a single opportunity to be there.

Debi would already be there with our children, following every chapter and verse our pastor taught. It was a time of dramatic growth for both of us—and for Debi, it was all new. She had never clearly heard about this profound love and grace, or the need to grow in trust and faith. And while I grew up hearing it on a regular basis, somehow it had never really registered.

Along with attending, we found ways of serving in our church. Both of us enjoy teaching Sunday school, and Debi has always had a particular gift for working with young children, leading them in Bible study, or helping tutor them after school. We also volunteered to help clean the church, and I took responsibility for shoveling snowy sidewalks in winter and mowing the lawns once a week for the rest of the year.

Our pastor would often see me and stroll across the grass to chat for a few minutes. In time, we fell into the habit of visiting over lunch in the church's kitchen. I developed a great respect for Pastor Curtis's character, knowledge of the Bible, and relationship with Christ. I asked him every question I could think of, and he would talk things through, show me relevant passages from the Scriptures, and sometimes recommend other books that could strengthen me in my faith. Over that kitchen table, he became a dependable mentor who did a great deal to help me "grow up" in my beliefs and understanding of God and the Bible.

My sister Linda and her husband, Jim, also became a big influence. Their example and encouragement really blessed us in those early years of our married life, amid all the hard work, parenting, and burgeoning faith. They showed us better ways of handling our money. We watched them raise five of their own children (three of whom became missionaries), and they helped us decide to homeschool our three youngsters—a choice that's had a far-reaching impact on our relationships with our children.

Mostly, Linda and Jim offered us a good, practical example of what it meant to be "saved": to let Christ completely transform your life, to make Him a part of everything—from marriage to parenting and from how we treat our customers to how we manage a business.

Debi and I tried to pass our slowly growing wisdom and our love for Christ on to our children, but we weren't as successful early on as we hoped. Jeremy, as he grew older, fell away from our faith, drifting in much the same way Debi and I had at his age. Though he'd been immersed in church services and activities, he had to find his own way. At one point, he bluntly rejected our beliefs and struck out on his own; like most young people, he had his adventures, made his mistakes, earned the scars of experience, and learned his hard lessons. And then— by the mercies of God—he did a complete 180 and came back to the Lord and to the faith we'd tried so hard to live before him.

One day, Debi opened a message he'd sent her from his home in California. "God's got a hold of me," it said. "And I wanted to tell you first, because I hurt you the most." There weren't any dry eyes in our house that day.

Today, Jeremy lives in Burbank, California, working with information technology, talking me through all the glitches in my computer, and raising his son (our only grandson). Like his sisters, he has been a great strength and encouragement to me through these last tumultuous years.

Jennifer took a different track. She was saved at a very young age with a perfectly clear understanding of what that meant and who Christ was. She never rebelled (to my knowledge) against anything and embraced her faith and the truth of God's Word wholeheartedly. After placing fifth in the Scripps National Spelling Bee as a child, she became involved as a teen with the ministry of Child Evangelism Fellowship. She has worked with the organization for many years in its Montreal office, where she puts her fluent French to excellent use in sharing Christ with Canadians.

Lisa, our youngest, was still pretty young when we opened Masterpiece Cakeshop, and she grew up in and around all the activities there. (I'll share more about that in the next chapter.) Like her sister, she held fast to her faith, but the events that followed our visit from David and Charlie had a profound impact on her life.

She realized, she told me later, that while she would have given them the same answer I did, if I hadn't been in the shop that day, she wouldn't really have understood the rationale for saying "no." She would have done it, she said, because she knew I would have done it—not because her own beliefs were so clear and grounded on the questions the incident raised.

That spurred her to study the Bible more deeply for herself and experience a great deal of growth in her own relationship with Christ. It's been a beautiful thing to see the impact maturing in her faith has had on every aspect of her life: her work, her relationships, and her mothering of her three little girls.

And so Debi and I give thanks and marvel. Three children—one who walked away from the Lord, one who sleepwalked through her faith for a while, and one who held fast and prayed for the others. Now, all three are close to Christ, to us, and to each other.

"I have no greater joy than to hear that my children are walking in the truth," the Apostle John wrote.[4] And I know exactly what he meant.

After I'd been at Golden Cream about five years, my good friend Ron suggested that I join him in applying for a position in the main bakery at King Soopers—a large grocery chain with a huge market in Denver. The pay and benefits, Ron said, would be a little better. I hesitated: God was indeed providing for all our needs, and Mr. Lee took very good care of his employees at Golden Cream. Besides, I really did love my job—the work, the pace, the people I worked with, even the product. I saw no compelling reason to change.

Ron's persistence, however, eventually wore me down. Maybe it was my ego. *Would a company as big and powerful as King Soopers consider someone like me? Am I good enough for the big leagues?* I finally headed down to the main facility to fill out the necessary forms. When I got to the space designated for "experience," I decided to get creative. I filled the space with everything I had learned to bake or cook. I didn't just write "mix cakes"; I elaborated: "I am familiar with a variety of cake batters, including different types of chocolate, white cake, yellow cake, applesauce spice…" On and on about my expertise with pie fillings and cookies, until I filled the space given and overflowed into the margins and then onto the back of the paper. If I had done it, I wrote it down.

My application must have stood out from the others. King Soopers called me the very next day. Two weeks later, I was holding a brand-new timecard.

My entire experience at King Soopers was new and different. For one thing, I hadn't worked a day shift in almost four years, so my sleep schedule was totally out of sync. My weekends also changed; at Golden Cream I'd worked Saturday nights through Thursday mornings, with unpredictable doses of overtime thrown in. At King Soopers, I was scheduled from Tuesday mornings through Saturday evenings.

The job description, however, was less predictable. I was now a "floater," meaning I no longer had a clearly defined role. I was simply assigned anywhere I was needed: stacking baskets of bread as packaged loaves came off the conveyor belts, loading those baskets into trailers to get them to the stores, cleaning flour dust from ceiling pipes (twenty feet above the floor), or even counting candles for inventory.

While counting candles one day, I had a confrontation with a union steward, who informed me that I was "working too hard" and that, with my lack of seniority, if anyone were to be laid off, it would likely be me. My reply was simple, honest, and to the point: I said I wasn't working for him or the union, or even King Soopers, for that matter. I was there to represent Jesus Christ and do it the best way I knew how. Furthermore, if I were laid off, that would be okay with me, as long as I were let go for doing something other than dishonoring My Lord. He shook his head and left me alone with my candles and my thoughts.

As it turned out, I only worked at King Soopers Bakery for about eighteen months before I was caught in a layoff precipitated by a different union issue.

While that issue was resolved within a few weeks, by then I was back at Golden Cream in my old job; they hadn't found anyone to take my place. It was good to be back.

Not that my time at King Soopers was wasted. Along with making many new friends, I was given an opportunity to work full-time in the cake decorating department for a few weeks—long enough for me to get my feet wet and solidify my vision of someday owning my own cake shop. Someday.

My opportunity to practice cake decorating at Soopers came along because a friend of mine had been hired to work in that same department. One day, back at Golden Cream, I asked her to help me design my first custom cake. It was not a beautiful thing to see, but apparently, she saw some promise, since she informed the department foreman that I had some artistic ability and experience and might be of use on the decorating team.

I remember clearly when that foreman came up to ask me, "So, I hear that you know how to decorate cakes?" I told him I had decorated before, but only a couple of cakes.

He decided to take a chance on me anyway. "Let's go over," he said, "and see what you can do."

We headed to the corner of the plant where the cake designers, a team of about thirty people, were decorating custom cakes. A few others were preparing the cakes for decorating or applying the preliminary icing. Still others checked the quality and accuracy of the designs and made sure the finished cakes were delivered to the proper stores.

And to think a year or two earlier that I hadn't even known custom cakes existed. Standing there that morning, I realized I was looking at my future.

9

Opening the Shop

As the years went by, Debi began nudging me more often about my long-deferred dream of opening my own cake shop. "When are you going to take that 'next step' you've always talked about?" she asked.

I learned early on to trust my wife's instincts—to believe in her love for me, and more than that, in her love for the Lord. I have found that He speaks to me, as often as not, through her and that it's a good thing to listen when He does. Especially when He's already been talking to me Himself along similar lines.

I used to ride the bus to and from my job, passing the long ride by reading. At that time, I'd taken to reading a lot of Civil War history and was especially bemused by what I was reading about General George McClellan. President Abraham Lincoln had chosen McClellan for the most crucial job of the war—leading the Union Army—and he wanted so much to believe in McClellan and let the man do his job. Only McClellan wouldn't do his job.

He was, by all accounts, a remarkable organizer. Nobody could get an army better armed and supplied, more effectively trained, and build up their morale for a fight like McClellan could. Trouble was, he didn't fight. He always thought he needed a few more men, a few more supplies, a little more information, a little more time before taking on the enemy. So he never quite got around to actually getting the fighting done in the way it would take to win the war.

Lincoln famously urged, encouraged, ordered, pleaded, begged, cajoled—everything he could think of to budge McClellan out of camp and into the field to aggressively pursue the enemy. He finally fired him, rehired him, and fired him again. Then along came Ulysses S. Grant—who was only so-so as an organizer but was a man who could and would give the enemy no quarter. He just went right at them and kept going at them like a bulldog in a bad mood.

"I can't spare this man," Lincoln is supposed to have said. "He fights."

Reading about all that, the conviction grew in my soul that I was more like McClellan than Grant. Twenty years down the road, I realized, I could still be sitting on this same bus, riding to and from the same job, making the same paycheck, no closer to making my dreams a reality. I didn't like that idea.

I wanted to follow Grant's example. He understood that, at some level, we're never prepared for what comes next. There's nothing we can ever do to be completely "ready." We do what we can with what we have and make it work.

I decided it was time to take action. I wanted to be someone God couldn't spare. I wanted to do what in my heart I knew He had made me to do.

It was time to open Masterpiece Cakeshop.

That turned out to be much more easily said than done.

For a while, I was making and selling custom cakes out of my own kitchen at home. The time came when I had to stop doing that. I called the Jefferson County Health Department to ask about getting a license to do more of that and was told, in no uncertain terms, that I couldn't. Licenses weren't issued, they said, for food preparation from a residence. And even if they were, zoning laws would restrict anyone from coming to my home to pick up the cake—I'd have to deliver each one. I quit creating cakes out of my house then and there.

Bit by bit, though, I began picking up more and more of the necessary tools and equipment at various auctions around the city. That included a monster oven, nearly as tall as I am—five feet across and four feet thick. Moving it proved a considerable adventure, but we finally stowed it with a friend who kindly kept it in his garage for well over a year, while other parts of my plan for opening Masterpiece fell into place. (I managed to find room in my own garage for another auction-bought monster, a seven-by-seven-by-three-foot freezer.)

By then, I'd left Golden Cream again and had been working for another company, Child's Pastry Shop, for nearly ten years. My boss at Child's, Mike Dixon, had done a great deal to expand my education, giving me not only plenty of experience designing custom cakes, but also trusting me to manage one of his shops for a while and giving me the opportunity to learn the intricacies of running a business.

Mike had also become a good friend. He knew how long I'd been nursing this dream of opening my own shop, and he never tried to talk me out of it. From time to time, he'd even invested generously in my coming independence. He gave me a small but durable mixer worth several hundred dollars, then later gave me a much, much larger one worth a couple thousand dollars.

These are the tools any full-time cake baker needs at his disposal, and I was a long way from being able to afford either one. Mike gave them, knowing one day I'd use them in a business competing with his. It was a wonderful kindness I've never forgotten.

Debi and I began spending our Sunday afternoons driving around town, checking out shopping centers and strip malls, looking for a suitable site for the shop. I began to realize that this was not going to be an easy task. A bakery needs certain electrical and plumbing accommodations, particular types of wall coverings, even unique ceiling tiles, to meet the abundance of health, building, and safety codes. We weren't finding anything promising, and one afternoon I told Debi the whole thing was beginning to seem impossible.

"Maybe God has an empty bakery available that we don't know about," she said. "One already set up with everything we need."

"No," I said. "I know about all the bakeries around, and there isn't anything like that anywhere near here."

Score one for Debi. Shortly after that, we happened on a bakery that had recently closed. The property was nearly perfect for us, and only a half mile from our home. And although that opportunity didn't work out in the end, I still felt more confident that God could and would find a way to provide exactly what we needed.

"Exactly what we needed" turned out to be a frozen yogurt shop, just five or six minutes from my house. We signed the lease and finally opened our doors on September 3, 1993.

It was so much fun to open that Friday morning,[1] even though it was probably the worst time of year to launch a shop dedicated to designing custom cakes. For one thing, it was the end of wedding-cake season, so we would have to survive for the first year without that valuable income. Not to mention that our shop was hidden in a nearly forgotten shopping center, with more than half of its storefronts vacant. At least there was plenty of parking. (For me, and for the friends who'd been storing all of my equipment in their garages.)

But I knew God had directed me to open a cake shop and that He had guided us to this very spot, if for no other reason than to prove He could help us be successful under such daunting circumstances—or enable us to serve Him, regardless of the outcome.

The night before the grand opening, I had pulled the first cakes out of my gigantic oven and set them in the huge freezer to cool. Next morning, I brought out the first one. I separated two layers of the white cake to spread raspberry filling, put the layers back together, and covered them with buttercreme icing. I decorated that with a beautiful arrangement of buttercreme flowers and was about to place the whole creation into the showcase when a man walked in, asking about a cake for his secretary. I showed him the one that I'd been working on and offered to add an inscription. He asked for "Happy Birthday." I piped it on, and a moment later, I rang up our shop's very first cake sale.

The man's name was Rod, and I congratulated him on being our first customer.

"You mean the first today?"

"The first ever! We just opened the store for business."

"The very first?"

"Yep. The very first!"[2]

I'll never forget the thrill of that sale. I was really in business. And my business was going to be designing cakes.

By the end of that day, we had about twenty-five to thirty transactions on the cash register—at least twenty of them from my sister's five kids. That didn't matter. We were open for business and selling cakes! I knew we could make a living doing this and make a life doing it too.

10

Masterpiece Cakeshop

Those of us who make a living baking—whether for a massive operation like Golden Cream or a fairly small shop like mine—know there is considerably more to the job than turning on the mixer and sliding another tray of cookies in and out of the oven. I don't want to bore you with all the details, but I would like to give you a quick glimpse of at least some of what's involved in making a cake shop work.

On average, I complete nine or ten custom-made, decorated cakes a day—some sheet cakes, some tiered. On Friday and Saturday, that number can easily jump to fifty or sixty cake creations. It's not unusual for me to create a hundred or more cakes a week on average.

During graduation season (and, in the old days, wedding season), those numbers can go up appreciably. Some days, I'm working virtually around the clock. The same holds true at Christmas, when we're usually deluged with orders for specialty and seasonal cakes. We're also especially busy in the week leading up to Thanksgiving each year, when for three or four days we switch to pies, just as a change of pace. (Thanksgiving just isn't so much a cake holiday.) We make about a hundred of those too.

That's on top of about 30 dozen frosted brownies a week, and maybe 120 dozen or so cookies, which our shop offers both individually and in "grab bags" of assorted flavors. I also try to keep about 30–40 "show cakes" on display inside and behind the counter to give potential customers a sampling of what we can do.

You learn psychology by providing customer service: people like to see a variety on display when they come through the door. They may only have come in wanting one brownie and a cup of coffee, but they find something wonderfully pleasing about taking in a whole spectrum of cake and cookie possibilities. They appreciate knowing they could buy a lot of things, whether they actually want to buy anything else today or not.

Providing all of those baked goods for them to look at requires a lot of sugar and flour and such. That means mixing about 200 pounds of batter a week during the "off season," and closer to 2,200 pounds a week during graduation months and the big holidays, as well as preparing all the icing needed to cover that batter once it's baked and has become a few dozen cakes.

Keeping those various goods streaming through production takes more than a little mental (and sometimes physical) juggling. You have to constantly remember how much of which ingredients you need for each creation—how much flour, butter, sugar, seasoning—when to mix each combination, and for how long. You're decorating one cake while keeping track of how long the next one has been in the oven and gauging how many cakes you can bake before the next batch of cookies needs to go in, how many brownies you can ice before the next rush hits, and how long you can help this customer before you need to excuse yourself to go take something out of the oven. It never stops.

And since each aspect of the job is fairly equally crucial—you can't neglect the customers while you're baking, can't give up too much of the decorating time to ringing up sales out front, can't get too busy icing one cake to check orders for the next dozen online—we always have a lot of balls in the air.

Keeping all of that on track, while producing quality products that are both delicious and creatively satisfying, takes a special skill set. For one thing, you have to be blessed with a lively imagination—not only for coming up with new ideas, but for implementing the ideas that customers bring you. That includes just about every imaginable combination of shape, size, color, and design.

Some examples:

For a local food distributor, I created an eight-by-twelve-foot cake modeled on their biggest warehouse, including the parking lot and cars out front. (The cake was built around a Styrofoam frame.) I also made a three-dimensional replica of Fred Flintstone's car, complete with tiger-skin top. I crafted an entire cake in the shape of a great pink rose.

Lisa and I love doing portraits, caricatures, and sculptures (she's especially good at portraits). It's just a particularly fun challenge to try capturing the spirit of a person from their habits, features, and personality.

Back in 1987, when the Denver Broncos were headed to their first Super Bowl in a decade, I made a large cake bust of quarterback John Elway, which sat on display in our shop during the week before the big game. (On Saturday, we took it down to the local children's hospital, where it was a big hit; the kids enjoyed eating Elway's head while watching him throw passes.)

I was especially honored to be invited to create a cake to honor Billy Graham at a celebration of his one-hundredth birthday at the Billy Graham Library in Charlotte, North Carolina. The theme was "Through My Father's Eyes," and I was able to create a portrait of Mr. Graham on the cake. Although Mr. Graham himself had passed away a few months before the event, it was a great blessing to be able to meet his son Franklin and other family members and to have that small part in recognizing one of the great Christian leaders of my lifetime.

Along similar lines, I was commissioned to create a cake in the design of a Wittenberg Bible, using a great deal of calligraphy and golden-edged "pages." I've made a host of teddy bear cakes (they were quite the rage for a while, back when I was working for Child's), tiered snowman cakes, images of every imaginable kind of animal, transportation, and sport. (Living among Broncos fans, I've made pretty much everything you can color orange and blue.)

Creating some of those cakes requires special skills that have nothing to do with baking at all, like knowing how to think about a picture, recognize the most crucial details, identify important contrasts of color and perspective, and reproduce those images in watercolor washes and frosting calligraphy. Most of those were not things I learned, for the most part, at Golden Cream or King Sooper's; I picked them up in those long-ago high school art classes, watching and listening to Mr. Filson and Mr. Glasgow.

From them, from Eddie at Golden Cream, from Mike Dixon at Child's, and from many others, I absorbed the importance of people skills, of knowing how to look customers in the eye and listen to their ideas…about what they want on a birthday cake, about how they feel about life. You can be a good baker standing back by the ovens, but you can't run a good shop unless you get to know the people who are buying and commissioning what you bake and design.

You also have to keep the place clean, the items looking fresh and tasty, the atmosphere relaxed and cheerful. You better make good coffee. You're blessed if you have a parent or a spouse who will take care of the bills and help schedule the deliveries while you're working up the latest artistic design or talking about the weather with the traveler who just stopped in.

It's a great deal of work, like anything rewarding usually is, and I've been doing it for about twelve hours a day, six days a week on average, for forty-five years—twenty-eight of them from my own shop. I can honestly say that in all that time, I've never had one day—not one single day—when I woke up and thought, *Not this again. I just don't feel like it today.* Nope. Never.

I'm one of those lucky folks who gets paid to do what he loves to do—who is rewarded tangibly and spiritually with the opportunity to stretch, deepen, and exercise my favorite talents for the joy, delight, and encouragement of other people. In fact, I'm not just lucky—I'm blessed and thankful beyond measure.

From the beginning, Debi and I laid down some ground rules. I wouldn't craft obscene messages. I wouldn't design a cake that would communicate something cruel or unkind or belittling to another person. I wouldn't create anything that mocked or contradicted my faith. I wouldn't use my talents to celebrate occasions I don't believe in (like Halloween). When the marijuana headshop down the mall from us asked me to make weed-shaped cookies, I declined. We also closed our doors on Sunday because the Bible teaches that God gave us the gift of one day out of seven to rest.

I also understood that starting a new business was going to mean long hours and a great deal of work. My parents had prepared me for that, modeling their own healthy work ethic for me and my siblings every day of our lives. (I only remember Dad missing a day for sickness once—and that was for tick fever.) From a fairly early age, my brothers and sisters and I were expected to do our chores and take seriously our responsibilities as members of a family. I grew up hoping to pass along those same expectations to our own children.

So from the beginning, I wanted my shop to be God's shop—He is the Master in "Masterpiece," and I am reminded of that every time I write the name "Masterpiece" out. That means a high standard of excellence and an environment in which anyone and everyone could feel welcome. I wanted to show my customers and my staff the same patience, kindness, and warmth I'd experienced growing up. I wanted to treat everyone the same—not based on their gender, the color of their skin, or the beliefs of their heart.

That's how I knew immediately—the day I opened the shop—that this place was going to be special. I was dedicated to serving everyone who came through our door in a way that made them feel seen, loved, and appreciated.

Even more than that, I wanted my shop to be a place where I connected with customers. Where, whenever possible, I could listen to them, get to know them, and put them at their ease. I wanted to be able to encourage people who perhaps needed something more than just a cookie and a cup of coffee. I also wanted to be able to share my faith when opportune moments came along.

Running a cake shop is no small task. The easiest thing from the beginning would have been to hire other people to handle everything out front and just concentrate my attention full-time on the baking and decorating in the back of the shop. But for me, the person-to-person aspects of what I do are as fulfilling, in their own way, as what I create on those custom cakes. That's why I make it a deliberate point to get out of the kitchen as much as possible—to smile, greet customers, maybe sit down with them for a few minutes, hear their stories—or at least the adventure of the morning or the weather prediction for the afternoon.

After almost three decades, some of those coming through the door have become old friends. They've been dropping in for a cupcake or a cup of coffee regularly for years; they came before all the events surrounding my court cases, and they've kept coming since.

The cases, of course, have brought in a whole different group of customers, some deliberately looking to make the acquaintance of "the guy who wouldn't make the cake," and others who just figure out who I am after they walk in and see me. Occasionally, they may ask for an autograph, but I am uncomfortable giving them—it makes it seem too much about me. But if they want to pose for a selfie (the new "autograph," as somebody called it), I will always oblige. There's something more neighborly, I guess, about being invited to share somebody's picture.

One of the special features of our cake shop is a large atlas I keep on hand. I originally bought it for occasions when I'm asked to draw a particular state or country on a cake. (You'd be surprised how often this happens.) Now I keep it up near the front door, and it's marked with the signatures and autographs of people who've come in from all over the world—forty-nine states (I'm still waiting for someone from Rhode Island) and at last count forty-three countries.

The nature of our location has changed over the years—and the mall where we originated is much busier than it used to be. It's situated in a way that's conducive to these drop-ins, many of them people who work in or frequent other places at the mall. We're across the parking lot from a gun shop and a couple of sports bars. At the far end of our building is a marijuana head shop. There's also a vape shop, and in the suite right next door is a massage parlor (but, I was told, "the legitimate kind"— whatever that means). It's an interesting neighborhood. Who'd have thought I'd be the most controversial tenant?

And then, down the way a bit, is where the Alcoholics Anonymous group meets. A lot of the people attending those meetings come by for a cookie or a piece of cake. These people really seem to care and look out for one another. On "birthdays"—anniversaries of their sobriety—they'll often send someone over to pick up some cookies or ask me to decorate a cake that celebrates the number of days or years that person's gone without a drink. (I think one of the reasons they like our shop is that they know I don't put any alcohol in my baked goods—another of the guidelines Debi and I decided before we opened it.)

I'm glad they're free to choose anything we offer without having to worry about what's in it. I want them to feel at ease in our shop.

In some ways, for me, Masterpiece Cakeshop is like a mission field. From the beginning, I've wanted it to be a place where God is made known and where everything we do and say, everything we create and sell, reflects well on Him. I don't put anything in that display case out front that I don't want my mom, my grandkids—or my Lord—to see. That's a primary reason for the great care I take in deciding what messages I will and will not communicate.

It's also the motivation for extending grace and a warm welcome to everyone who walks through the door.

Those were the dreams I had when I started the business. And, happily, we've been blessed to see our hopes and plans come abundantly true.

As I said, some people have been coming to our shop for years; we're their go-to for special occasions, and they return again and again to ask for something new for this year's birthday or anniversary. After all these years of doing this, I find myself making birthday and graduation cakes for the children of people whose wedding cakes I made a few years ago. In some cases, I was making birthday cakes for the bride or groom long before the two of them ever met.

Those opportunities are rewarding and special, and so are the relationships I've been able to cultivate with people who've been coming through for years, sipping our coffee, nibbling on something sweet, and making themselves at home—just the way we want them to.

It's fun to meet new people, a joy to still be serving customers who long ago became friends, and a delight to still be flexing and stretching my God-given talents, trying new things and thriving on the creative challenge.

Some of the greatest pleasures of owning my own business have been the pleasant surprises that I couldn't have foreseen when I first opened these doors.

For one, my cake shop gave me the opportunity to know my father better. He had always been a good dad, a hard worker, and an encourager to me and my siblings. He hit baseballs with us and played catch, took us on regular picnics, and now and then took us fishing up at Evergreen Lake, one of his favorite spots.

He was enthusiastic about my idea for the cake shop, and once we opened for business, he became one of my regulars. He came in almost every morning, and I'd get a muffin for him and pour a cup of coffee. He befriended many of the customers that came in, and I was always proud to see him sitting there, chatting with someone new.

As weeks and months went by and these daily conversations became our enjoyable habit, he gradually opened up to me about some things he never had before—sharing memories of my childhood, of his childhood, of some of the horrors and heroism he saw in WWII during the Battle of the Bulge and the liberation of Buchenwald. Sometimes we talked politics, sometimes baseball, and sometimes about his bouts as a one-time Golden Glove boxer.

And in return, he gave me new opportunities to share with him—to talk over some of my joys and disappointments, the struggles of the new business, the pleasures and challenges of being a parent to my own three children.

He passed away a few years ago, but I cherish the memory of his deep love for his family and all those wonderful conversations over all those cups of coffee.

The cake shop also revealed over time the hidden gifts and creativity of my youngest daughter, Lisa. She was just thirteen years old when we opened the shop, and growing up, she was always a little fascinated by what I could do with cakes—the intricacy of the designs and the smooth, selective application of the frosting. That fascination only grew after she eventually came to work in the shop, began helping behind the counter, and had the day-by-day chance to see those creations coming to fruition.

That could have been nothing more than a "gee whiz, my dad's good at that" kind of enthusiasm. But Lisa herself was always pretty artistic and was never content to just watch me do what I do. She wanted a chance to do it herself. One day, she announced her desire to take a crack at cake designing, and we made room at the counter for her to see what she could do. She took to it like a duck to water.

Lisa now works side-by-side with me, swapping out brushes, brainstorming designs, and creating her own custom cakes that my customers enjoy at least as much as they do mine. It's a marvel and a pleasure for me to watch her work, exercising the beautiful talent God has given her. (It's good to have the help too.) And often enough, those are our times, working in the back of the shop together, talking through our memories and thoughts on life the way Dad and I used to discuss his and mine, sitting at a table out front.

Even my grandkids are starting to show some artistic abilities, gradually learning bits of what we do and how we do it, sometimes experimenting a little at decorating little cakes we provide for them to play with and practice on.

It's all been part of the blessing of building up this business together as a family.

Isn't it something? You make your plans, save for your dream, jump through all the "hoops" that stand between you and that wonderful ideal you've been nurturing in your mind. You take that big step—make the dream a reality—and you think you know why you're doing it: to support your family, to make a living doing what you most love to do, to contribute a little to the community, to honor your God.

And then He surprises you. He not only brings it all together in beautiful ways, but also adds layer upon layer of blessings that you never saw coming.

That's what Masterpiece Cakeshop has been for me.

11

The Legal Challenge

little more than six weeks had passed since David and Charlie came into my store, hoping I'd create their wedding cake. Despite the two parking-lot protests early on, the flurry of media coverage, and the unrelenting abuse of phone calls and threats, nothing major had come of the awkward discussion about the cake.

Nothing, at least, to make me think this was more than an unpleasant storm that would soon blow over and leave me to run my shop in peace.

Then, one Tuesday in September, I found in the morning mail a legal-size envelope bearing the state seal of Colorado. Inside I found a letter from the Colorado Civil Rights Division.

It's funny what changes your life: Sitting down with a new customer. Answering a phone. Opening a letter.

Even as I opened the envelope—instinctively knowing this was probably bad news—I felt, in some quiet back corner of my mind, a small sigh of relief. No more wondering. No more limbo. What I was about to read would finally give me a clue to where this was going, once and for all.

It did. The letter informed me that, based on a complaint by David, the state was formally charging me with sexual-orientation discrimination. Officials said I had violated the Colorado Anti-Discrimination Act by treating David and Charlie differently than other customers on the basis of their personal characteristics.

That I had offered to sell these two men anything else in my store didn't seem to matter. That I had declined their request based not on their personal characteristics, but the message they had asked me to communicate, also appeared to be irrelevant.

Ten days later, I received a second notice from the Civil Rights Division citing a second charge filed against me—this one by Charlie. As in the first letter, state officials informed me that, based on these charges, the division would be conducting a formal investigation of my actions in relation to the incident.

A few months later, I received a third letter. This one informed me that, based on the results of that investigation, the state was referring the charges to the Colorado Civil Rights Commission—a panel of seven gubernatorial appointees who review and rule on cases the division's investigators refer to them—for prosecution. I don't remember anyone calling or visiting the shop to ask me any questions; the "investigation" apparently hadn't required any information or participation from me at all. I was directed to appear before an administrative law judge, where I would be prosecuted by attorneys from the same Civil Rights Commission that would be ruling on my case.

In other words, the prosecutors and the judges were virtually one and the same. That seemed more than a little unfair, since it basically ensured I had no chance of winning the legal argument.

Things were suddenly happening very fast—and I knew these legal riptides were carrying me way out beyond my depth.

What I didn't know was that this was the beginning of a case that would make legal history—and ultimately affect not only my own civil rights and religious freedom, but potentially that of every American.

I marveled that a legal battle this big would be joined over cakes. Surely there were bigger legal "hills to die on." A battle over the right to publish classified information, maybe...over leading worship in a public place...over posting controversial viewpoints on the internet. Those I could see. But cakes?

It was only the beginning of a new surge in legal prosecutions of Christian artists and business owners who opted to live out their faith beliefs in their workplace. Soon enough, God was using not only cakes to draw attention to this growing infringement on personal liberties, but also floral designs. Wedding films and photography. T-shirt designs. Private devotional books.

These cases, each of which involved the legal defense of "rights of conscience," gradually began attracting massive media attention all over the country—not because the people involved were famous or wealthy or looking for some time in the spotlight. I know many of them, and they're just ordinary folks, like me, who suddenly found themselves faced with a crucial decision: whether they would, or would not, hold fast to their deepest beliefs and convictions.

Some people believe that "every man has his price." But I've heard it said that that's not always true—that more often, "every man has a line." A line in his (or her) soul that he will not, cannot bring himself to cross— no matter what. These so-called "conscience cases" are about people who, like me, woke up one morning to find that they'd come to their line.

I wasn't looking to become a public figure or a cause célèbre when I sat down at my desk that afternoon with David and Charlie. I had no idea I was stepping up to a line that would basically bisect my whole life, dividing it forever between what happened before and what's happened since that quiet summer day.

But the moment they spoke, I knew in my heart what my answer would have to be.

So what do you know? God worked in the quiet life and mundane circumstances of a Colorado cake designer to bring a national issue out into the light.

It reminds me sometimes of a passage from the Bible, 1 Corinthians
1:26–27:

> For you see your calling, brethren, that not many wise accord-
> ing to the flesh, not many mighty, not many noble, are called.
> But God has chosen the foolish things of the world to put to
> shame the wise, and God has chosen the weak things of the
> world to put to shame the things which are mighty. . . .

I am often a foolish, weak fellow. But then it wasn't going to be my
wisdom, or my strength, I was leaning on in the great battle that was fast
shaping up before me.

12

The Thing about Weddings

My decision in the shop that summer afternoon—and my continuing decision to stand by it ever since—has likely cost me at least tens of thousands of dollars in revenue and eight years and counting of physical threats to my family, insults to my character, and untold hours tied up in legal action of one form or another.

I'm sure there's an excellent chance that you're wondering, *What on earth is this guy's thing about marriage? Is it really that big a deal? Is it really worth all of this pain and aggravation?* Or, as many people have put it, *Why not just bake the cake?*

As I've already said, my hesitation was not about the men who made the request. My objection is never to the person who is asking me to create a cake with a particular message. My objection—in this case—is to the message itself. I can and cheerfully will serve anyone. I cannot and will not communicate every message.

I mentioned earlier that I have demurred from creating a lot of non-wedding cakes. I don't do Halloween cakes, for instance. I personally cannot see Jesus celebrating that day or encouraging me to do so, especially if the motivation is to glorify things the Bible so explicitly condemns.

Early on in my cake design career, someone close to me came in asking for a cake with a specific design. Flipping through a reference book for a picture to base the design on, I found out the symbol was occultic. Across the page from the requested emblem was a drawing of an elephant. *I'd rather do anything else—even the elephant on that page—than the occult design on this one,* I thought.

Soon after, the person requesting the cake dropped by, and I gently explained why I couldn't create anything with the symbol she'd asked for. She shrugged, said she certainly understood, and then thought for a second.

"Well—how 'bout an elephant?" she said. Another time that God proved to me that He was in control of every aspect of my life.

So from the beginning, the message has been important to me. I think that's true of any artist. No one who takes art seriously does his work on the assumption that no one else will really notice or pay any attention to it. Why work and discipline yourself to become the best you can possibly be at a skill or talent whose result no one cares about?

I have no illusions of being in the same league with regard to cakes that Michelangelo was in carving statues and painting ceilings, that Shakespeare was in crafting sonnets and plays, or that even Norman Rockwell was in creating magazine covers for the *Saturday Evening Post.* But I do have this much in common with each of those guys, and with every other artist who ever lived or worked, whatever his medium.

Number One: I take my art seriously. Number Two: I want others to appreciate it. And Number Three: I want that work to communicate a clear message to those who do take time to appreciate it.

If I succeed at Number Two, then there's no way I fail at Number Three. No one takes time to really appreciate the work of an artist only to say, "Yep. There's something that doesn't mean anything at all." They may not understand what the art means. They may not like what it means. They may not agree with what it means. But they'll know that the person who assembled that creation had a definite idea in mind and had at least some sense of what that idea was all about.

"Jack," you're still saying. "It's just a cake. Nobody's thinking anything other than 'That looks tasty,' or 'I hope it's red velvet.'"

But that's just not true. Especially of a wedding cake.

Think about all the other elements that go into a wedding ceremony. Many offer options. The flowers—white roses, or red, or maybe orchids, or gardenias? The readings that are chosen—from the Bible, from the poets, from something the groom's sister wrote? The vows—the usual, or something the bride and groom composed for themselves?

Inevitably, that carries over to the reception: how formal or not, what sort of decorations, what kinds of songs are played and probably danced to. And then, of course, the cake.

Everybody knows a wedding cake when they see one.

And most can tell, upon closer examination, whether this cake was custom-designed especially for this bride and groom. They can see how much artistry went into the creation. They'll sense the celebration and perhaps see in the design something exceedingly personal, something beautifully reflecting the unique love and relationship between these two people. If it's done well enough, they may even invite someone else to come up and see it too. Many will ask, "Who made the cake?"

But whatever their thoughts on the cake itself, at least two messages are instantly, invariably communicated when people look at a wedding cake.

A marriage has taken place.

And that marriage should be celebrated.

As a cake designer, I want to do both of those things. I want to create the cake my customers have requested into something delightful, something delicious, something that celebrates this wonderful coming together of these two unique souls. But to communicate that, I have to believe in the message: that this is a marriage that should take place and that should be celebrated.

That goes directly to what I believe about marriage itself.

And what are those things?

Well, for one thing, I believe marriage was ordained by God. The Bible teaches that God is the One who came up with the marriage idea—early on, in the Garden of Eden[1]—and He had some very specific intentions in mind when He did so. Genesis 2:24 tells us: "Therefore a man shall leave his father and mother and be joined to his wife, and they shall become one flesh."

Jesus Himself affirms this:

> And He answered and said to them, "Have you not read that He who made them at the beginning 'made them male and female,' and said, 'For this reason a man shall leave his father and mother and be joined to his wife, and the two shall become one flesh'? So then, they are no longer two but one flesh. Therefore, what God has joined together, let not man separate."[2]

Those passages tell me several crucial things about marriage.

Once again, this union was God's idea, and He takes it seriously. Marriage is a sacred thing.

Two, that He intended it to be a one-of-a-kind relationship—the physical, emotional, and spiritual union of one man to one woman. (There is no biblical passage that mentions or allows for same-sex marriage.)

Three, that He designed marriage to be a pure and permanent commitment. That doesn't mean divorce is impossible, but it shouldn't be so easy or so common that people end up taking marriage lightly.

All those ideas are magnified and illuminated in a famous New Testament passage, Ephesians 5:22–33, which says:

> Wives, submit to your own husbands, as to the Lord. For the husband is head of the wife, as also Christ is head of the church; and He is the Savior of the body. Therefore, just as

the church is subject to Christ, so let the wives be to their own husbands in everything.

Husbands, love your wives, just as Christ also loved the church and gave Himself for her, that He might sanctify and cleanse her with the washing of water by the word, that He might present her to Himself a glorious church, not having spot or wrinkle or any such thing, but that she should be holy and without blemish.

So husbands ought to love their own wives as their own bodies…let each one of you in particular so love his own wife as himself, and let the wife see that she respects her husband.

Whole books have been written on that passage, and this is not the place for me to explore all the theology of the Bible, or even to explain all the thoughtful elements of these verses. But the main point, I believe, is pretty clear: Marriage is not some casual thing, nor is it simply a convenient institution for any two people who happen to love each other. God designed marriage for His own specific purposes, and He directs the relationship of a husband and wife within marriage to illustrate His own relationship with those who commit their lives to Him.

When we mess up marriage—by treating it as less than sacred, by treating our spouse in unkind and unloving ways, or by twisting the relationship itself into something it isn't—we're not just destroying our own happiness. We're misrepresenting God to those around us. We're painting an inaccurate and unflattering portrait of what His love for each of us looks like.

And that's just not a message I'm willing to help communicate. There are too many people out there already who have a hard enough time understanding God or believing His love for them. I'm not willing to use my talents to make it that much harder for them to believe.

"Okay," you may be saying, "that's fine for you, Jack, but I really don't take the Bible all that seriously. That's just not my understanding of what marriage is or has to be."

I understand that. My beliefs don't have to be your beliefs. But my beliefs are what make me who I am. My commitment to God and to the truth of a book I believe to be His holy Word is the defining premise of my life, the focus of my faith, and the guiding directive for my actions.

If you ask me to separate all of that from my work, from my decisions, from my art...I simply can't do that. Not just won't—*can't*. It's like asking a contractor to build a great building, but first remove the foundation.

Where do we think artistic creativity comes from? Something outside of ourselves? Of course not. It's water from the fountain of our soul. It comes from that deep-down place inside each of us where our experiences, our understanding, our intuitions, and our deepest beliefs and convictions about life all stir together. Those can't be separated from each other any more than you can sift out the various ingredients from a cake after it's baked.

That's why I say that I'll serve any person, but I won't communicate all messages. Serving people is merely about recognizing each individual as a person worthy of respect who is made in the image of God. I'm not trying to force any person to see the world the way I do or to embrace my beliefs about God and the Bible. If you want to reject Jesus and purchase a cupcake, go ahead. I'll gladly sell you that cupcake and a cup of coffee to go with it, maybe even engage you in a conversation about our differences.

But asking me to draw on my creativity to communicate a message I believe is wrong? That's asking me to stop being me. To change my own relationship with the Lord. To deny the deepest convictions of my heart and pretend I haven't learned the most difficult lessons of my life, or that they don't matter. That's not something any person has the right to ask of another.

Or a command any government has the right to force one of its citizens to obey.

13

Taking On the Government

Many, many people have asked about my views on marriage, about why I don't "just bake the cake." Something I'm asked less often—but even by people who understand my circumstances and agree with my stand—is about my attitude toward the government.

Some wonder how a believer in Christ can bring himself to defend himself in court, even against the government.[1] Others assume I have a deep hatred, at this point, for the government officials who've done so much to make my life so difficult.

Well, as I've said many times, I don't hate anyone—not David and Charlie, not those who've served on the Colorado Civil Rights Commission, not the judges who've ruled against me at various points along the way, and not those who've elected to file additional complaints about me in the aftermath of my original case. Hatred, on my part, has nothing to do with any of this.

Christians who've spent time in the Bible know that the same Scriptures that teach us to love our neighbor urge us to respect our government and its leaders. The Apostle Paul offers this directive:

> Give everyone what you owe him: If you owe taxes, pay
> taxes; if revenue, then revenue; if respect, then respect; if
> honor, then honor.[2]

At first glance, that passage might make it sound as though I'm
going against the Bible in challenging my state's actions toward me.
That is certainly not my intention. I recognize the truth that Paul lays
out: that no government comes to power without God's allowing it to
do so.[3] I pay my taxes, I pray for our leaders, I participate conscientiously in civic life (mostly by voting), I observe the health code and
stop at red lights, and I try to not only obey the letter but honor the
spirit of the law.

The legal impasse that has brought me into conflict with the government is not grounded—for my part—in anger, or a desire for vengeance,
or a determination to obey some laws and ignore others as it suits me.
In fact, if anything, I have reasons (lawsuits aside) to particularly appreciate government officials in the state of Colorado.

A few years ago, I took an old van I hadn't used in a while in for emissions testing. I'd decided to renew the plates and get it out on the
road again. The van, however, flunked the test, leaving me unsure what
to do. With more than two hundred thousand miles on the odometer, I
was looking at spending a lot of money to get it back into usable shape—
more than I really wanted (or had on hand) to spend. And it was probably more than anyone else would want to invest in such a massive
overhaul either, so selling it didn't seem like a good prospect. That left
junking the old machine and buying something new.

Before I could do that, though, I received another letter in the mail
from state officials. I'd grown pretty wary of these, after all the formal
complaints and multiple summons I'd received, but this one turned out
to be an invitation to participate in a program the state was sponsoring
for certain vehicles than had flunked emissions. They wanted to run some
tests for a few weeks and offered to pay for a rental car if I brought the

old, worn-out van in and left it with state-designated mechanics. I was happy to do that.

Once the test period was over, I went to retrieve my ancient van...only to find that the state had opted to repair and replace everything related to the emissions problem—free of charge. ("Is this the same state that is suing you?" my sister asked in disbelief.) It was a good reminder that God does use government authorities to accomplish some positive things in our lives.

Then the state did me another big favor. At one crucial point during the course of my case, a local radio station asked to broadcast all day long from our cake shop, and my family and I made a lot of arrangements to prepare for it. Not long before the big event, though, I received a jury summons in the mail—for the day of the broadcast.

Ordinarily, I'm glad to comply with a summons and look forward, as I said, to doing my civic duty. But this was terrible timing, even if it turned out to be for just one day—a day I really needed to be on hand at the shop. I didn't even want to think about being impaneled on a jury for days or weeks in the middle of everything going on at the time with our case.

A couple of nights before I was scheduled to serve, I called the court to see if I was required to appear. As I dialed, I prayed. The automated voice reeled off the numbers of the groups who did and didn't have to show—and to my great relief, I was excused. (Just to be sure, I read the numbers aloud to Debi to confirm it too.) I was free to go to work, and the radio event went beautifully, drawing a large, friendly crowd of supporters to the shop—hundreds of people coming by to offer prayers and support and encouragement. A wonderful day—a day to remember.

A week or two later, though, I received another of those dreaded official government letters in the mail. This one cited me for failing to appear for jury duty.

I called to straighten things out, explaining to someone on the court-house phone that I had called and had been excused. The lady asked for the date in question.

"Oh, that day," she said, when I told her. "Our computers were messed up that day." Seems those who were supposed to come in on the given morning were all accidentally excused, and vice versa.

This, I believe, is why the Bible tells us "to be anxious for nothing" and to pray about everything.[4] You never know when the Lord's gracious mercies are going to extend all the way down to a computer program.

In the verses from Romans quoted earlier, there's that line near the end about rendering "to all their due." The government has reasonable expectations of its citizens: that we pay our taxes and customs duties, that we respect elected officials and law enforcement officers, that we "honor the office" and what it stands for—even if we have our personal qualms about the person filling the role.

But if I am to render what I justly owe, it stands to reason that I don't have to render what I don't justly owe. And one thing I don't justly owe the government is authority over my conscience. I recognize the right of government officials to determine school zones and speed limits and tax rates and the voting age. I don't recognize their right to tell me what to think and believe, because it doesn't exist. (The First Amendment to the U.S. Constitution protects our consciences from government control.)

Jesus referenced this idea when He famously told the Pharisees, "Render unto Caesar what is Caesar's, and unto God what is God's."[5] To a certain extent, and under certain circumstances, my material possessions and even my body are at the service of the government. But my soul answers only and always to the Creator Who made it.

So whatever authority Colorado state officials may have over certain aspects of Masterpiece Cakeshop, in the end, God has final authority when it comes to deciding what messages I can or cannot communicate with the experience, tools, and artistic creativity at my disposal. And frankly, that seems to drive some of our officials crazy.

But—crazy or not—they chose to violate my constitutional right to freely hold, practice, and exercise my faith. To violate my freedom of speech by compelling me to communicate a message I disagree with. To enforce the laws in question with prejudice—treating me differently than others accused of the same offense. And to deny me a fair hearing—showing hostility toward my faith and toward me.

To all appearances, those violations are based primarily on contempt for my religious faith and Bible-based beliefs. And to my mind, all those unjust violations compromise the validity of their judgments in God's eyes.

Later in the Romans 13 passage I referenced earlier, the Apostle Paul directs believers to:

> Owe no one anything except to love one another, for he who loves another has fulfilled the law.... Love does no harm to a neighbor; therefore love is the fulfillment of the law.[6]

I have shown love in my attitude toward David and Charlie. I did not say—and I still haven't said—anything unkind against either of them because I didn't and don't feel any enmity toward them. I just disagreed with the message they hoped I would communicate. I understand they were disappointed, but they could easily have found any number of other nearby cake designers willing and able to express their desired message. In fact, I read that they eventually received a free cake and were offered other cakes for free.

Equally important is the fact that a government that has the power to force me to express messages I disagree with actually harms all Americans. No government should have that kind of power.

So by biblical standards, I feel that I have been obedient to the spirit of the law. By constitutional standards, I feel that I have been obedient to the letter of the laws of my nation and my state. And yet the government continued to pursue me, prosecute me, and persecute me.

That is my contention with the government, and so—while I will continue to pay taxes, vote, and even serve on a jury, if asked—I also will continue to explore every legal means of defending my rights and character...not just for my own sake, but for the sake of future generations.

14

The Hammer Falls

On Monday, the fourth day after my encounter with David and Charlie—and after two and a half crazy days of hate-filled phone calls—I was surprised to see "Focus on the Family," the name of the influential Christian ministry based about an hour away in Colorado Springs, pop up on my caller ID. But my first thought wasn't, *Great! Focus is calling!* It was, *Can they fake this?* I honestly don't think I'd had a single positive call since Thursday afternoon.

But the caller turned out to be Steve Jordahl, a reporter with *Family News in Focus*, the ministry's radio news program. Steve told me he'd heard about my situation over the weekend and asked if he could come to the shop the next day to interview me.

I was familiar with the show, and hearing Steve's friendly voice was a welcome relief from all the hostile calls I'd been getting. He caught me at a good time: by then, I was more than ready to share my side of the story and explain what had happened and my reasons for what I'd done.

Steve spent most of the next morning at my shop, seeing the set-up, learning my background, listening as I shared my faith. He understood where I was coming from, and it felt good to be able to talk through my beliefs in a way I hoped his listeners would identify with and respect.

Steve was more intuitive than me; he already sensed I was headed for a serious legal challenge. He said as much at the conclusion of our interview as he turned off his recorder and slid it to the side.

"There are organizations that can help in a situation like this—" he said.

"That's good news," I said.

"—and they can do it for free."

"That's even better," I said, smiling.

"And I can connect you with one."

I pushed his phone toward him. "Call 'em up!"

Without further ado, he picked up his phone and called a friend of his at Alliance Defending Freedom (ADF), an international legal ministry with a growing reputation for successfully defending Christians being prosecuted for living out their faith.

He put me on the phone with Greg Scott, who was at that time the senior director of media relations. Greg listened thoughtfully, then asked me quite a few questions (almost as many as Steve had). Clearly, he was trying to learn everything he could about me—not just every detail of what had happened in the shop, but about who I was and what I really believed. I told him all I could. One question seemed particularly crucial to him:

"Your decision had nothing to do with their sexual orientation?"

"No," I said, recounting my conversation with them, and reiterating the difference between selling them anything but not being willing to communicate a message I couldn't support. When I finished, he told me he was confident that ADF could and would take my case, should it turn out I had one. If I heard anything from the state, he said, I shouldn't respond, but should call ADF and let them handle it.

Getting back to work that afternoon, I marveled at the Lord's goodness—providing me out of nowhere with two men who gave me so much kind and tangible encouragement...even if my situation never did turn out to have any dire legal percussions.

A few days later, He sent me even more encouragement.

My daughter Lisa came into the kitchen where I was working to tell me a woman was out front, asking to meet with me. "Says she's some kind of attorney."

I set aside my project and went out to meet her.

"Hello," I said. "How can I help you?"

"You're Jack Phillips," she replied. "My name is Nicolle Martin. I'm an allied attorney with Alliance Defending Freedom. I heard about what was going on and decided I'd drop by and see if I could help."

We talked for a while. I soon realized that Nicolle, like Steve Jordahl and Greg Scott, was expecting my troubles to go far beyond angry phone calls and some negative media coverage. They really expected this to become a full-fledged lawsuit. As far as they were concerned, it was only a matter of time before I'd be going to court, probably to face off with officials of my own state. And when—not if—that happened, ADF was fully committed to representing me.

It was a great comfort, knowing that God was out in front of all that, bringing me the resources and support I would need before I even realized I would need them. I would have been even more encouraged if I'd known then what I learned about a year later.

Back in those first weeks, so much was happening so fast. I just assumed that Nicolle Martin's reaching out to me was connected with Steve Jordahl's kindly SOS to ADF and my conversation with Greg Scott. So, many months later, when Steve asked for a second interview, I naturally mentioned it to Nicolle.

She looked puzzled. "Who is Steve Jordahl?" she asked.

"The one who connected us in the first place," I told her.

"No one 'connected' us," she said. "I heard about your story and came over, on my own, to see if I could help. It looked like you needed it."

I didn't know it at that time, but I did need it. More than that, God knew I needed it. His sovereignty over my situation was complete. He was gently preparing me for the storm building just beyond the horizon, letting me know that the burden of what was coming would be on Him, not me.

A little more than a month after I enlisted Nicolle as my volunteer attorney, I received notice of the legal complaints filed by David and Charlie.

Once the Colorado Civil Rights Division finished its investigation (which didn't include me), made the charges official, and recommended that the Civil Rights Commission move forward in prosecuting the complaint, Nicolle filed our response. In keeping with Colorado civil law, the case was assigned to an administrative law judge for review. At this point the American Civil Liberties Union (ACLU) intervened on behalf of David and Charlie.

Nicolle filed our motion for summary judgment—which meant asking the judge to issue his ruling based on general facts agreed to by the two parties without going to a full-fledged trial. If I lost, I could face stiff penalties—fines, cease-and-desist orders, even up to a year in jail for each charge (though that aspect of the law was later removed). That prospect was sobering, but we thought it must be pretty clear that my choice not to create the wedding cake hinged on the message of the cake, not David or Charlie as individuals.

Apparently, that wasn't clear at all.

On December 6, 2013, Nicolle called to tell me the judge had ruled I did *not* have the freedom to choose the messages I use my artistic talents to express. Under the state's public accommodation law, the judge said, I was obliged (as a cake artist for hire) to express certain messages—even if doing so forced me to compromise my own beliefs about a given message. The state regarded that violation of my conscience as collateral damage—regrettable but not that big a deal.

My First Amendment protections, the judge said, couldn't trump the customers' right to my services. If I wouldn't contribute my creativity voluntarily, the state would compel me to create whatever message the customer asked for.

With that, he referred the case back to the Civil Rights Commission for sentencing.

On May 30, 2014, in the beautiful chambers of the old Colorado Supreme Court, the commission decided my case. From the expressions on their faces, the commissioners were enjoying the formal atmosphere, sitting in the high tribunal chairs. It was my first glimpse of a group whose words and decisions would greatly impact the next few years of my life and my first glimmer of the deep contempt with which they held both me and my beliefs as a Christian.

My case continued to draw considerable attention both locally and nationally, and droves of media came out for the hearing. When it came, it was blunt and harsh.

If I made wedding cakes at all, the commission ruled, I would have to make them for all occasions—even same-sex weddings. Even, for that matter, if the cake included some other design or wording or pornographic image that I found offensive. (Sadly, I do get requests for those kinds of cakes.) In effect, my government was ordering me to ignore my own faith and violate my conscience—to knuckle under or get out of the wedding industry.

What's more, for the next two years, the commissioners required me to file reports on every cake I declined to make, detailing who the would-be customer was and my reasons for choosing not to bake that particular cake, whether it was Halloween, obscenity, a cake with alcohol, a message denigrating a certain group or individual, or another request for something that violated my religious faith. I had to justify my every moral decision to the state of Colorado.

The only good news was that the commissioners didn't choose to fine me. Instead, they ruled (as required under the law) that my staff (including my daughter and my eighty-eight-year-old mother) would have to undergo mandatory reeducation—"sensitivity training," it's called. The price of remaining in business was that I had to teach my employees—primarily my own family—that I was wrong to operate my business in ways consistent with my faith in Christ.

Hearing all this for the first time, I really began to understand not only how much was at stake for my own life and work, but for other people of faith all over the country.

If the state could so blithely set aside my First Amendment rights, it could set aside theirs too.

If they could penalize me this severely for what I believed in my heart, then no one else's conscience or beliefs were any safer than mine.

What my government was suggesting—to me and to anyone else paying attention—was that a person's religious beliefs and conscience convictions cease to apply once that person arrives at his place of work. That posed a profound threat to every citizen's religious liberty, as well as to every individual's freedom of speech and expression.

Under Colorado law, the commission's draconian punishment had to be approved by the administrative law judge, but I had no doubt he would uphold it. The whole situation seemed unfair, with the commission acting as both prosecutor and final judge on my actions. The moment I was deemed worthy of prosecution, the ultimate ruling seemed pretty much a foregone conclusion. And sure enough, the commission ruled against me.

Reluctantly, I stopped creating wedding cakes. I had no doubt that many who shared the commissioners' sensibilities would be watching for opportunities to catch me declining other couples' requests, and those decisions would only lead to further complaints. Answering those complaints would quickly consume too much of my time. I had to let that precious part of my work at the cake shop go, for the time being.

As for the rest, well…maybe my case just fell through the cracks. Maybe everyone thought someone else would follow up to make sure my punishments were being meted out. Maybe, given that most of the commissioners weren't lawyers themselves, they didn't understand what bureaucratic steps were needed to enforce their directives. Or maybe they were just content with having slapped me around in front of the media and thought all their mandates would intimidate me into backing down and "playing ball."

But their ruling opened a remarkably big legal can of worms.

15

Cruelty and Contempt

We determined to file for an exception challenging the administrative court's decision (and by extension, the punishment the Civil Rights Commission suggested). For that, Nicolle was joined by another ADF attorney. They requested a stay on the actions the court ordered—the reeducation, the reports on declined cakes—but were denied. (A "stay" is a suspension of the punishments dictated by a legal body, pending a final decision in that case.)

On July 25, 2014, the two of them represented me before a second gathering of the Civil Rights Commission. Not only did the commissioners deny our request for an exception, but they also exposed even more clearly how deeply they despised my perspective and the faith I stood for. I felt that, clearly, most of them had convinced themselves that I was a bigot, that my bigotry was a direct result of my faith, and that no punishment was too severe for someone who dared to disagree with their own convictions about marriage and religious belief.

One commissioner, Diann Rice, put it this way:

"Freedom of religion and religion has been used to justify all kinds of discrimination throughout history, whether it be slavery, whether it be the Holocaust...I mean, we can list hundreds of situations where freedom of religion has been used to justify discrimination. And to me it is one of the most despicable pieces of rhetoric that people can use—to use their religion to hurt others."[1]

None of the other commissioners expressed any objection to that statement, and it drew support online from people who shared her point of view. In fact, a woman who had gone on Twitter years earlier to label me a "hater" was appointed a few years after this to serve alongside her on the commission.

The rulings and comments all hurt me in various ways. They forced me to choose between creating wedding cakes with messages I didn't agree with and not making any wedding cakes at all. While the choice itself was not difficult (I knew what the right thing was to do), it came at substantial cost.

Overnight, I lost my wedding income, which at the time was a significant percentage of my business. The loss of such a major portion of my business meant that many of those who worked with me—including close friends and even family members—had to go find other jobs. I didn't ask them to do that—they just knew there wouldn't be enough work for them to do now, nor enough money for me to pay them. When they left, I also lost the unique camaraderie that creative people share—working together, bouncing their ideas off each other, delighting in each other's handiwork.

The ruling also sullied my reputation in the community, implying that I was a bigot and that my faith was either a cover for that or the polluted fountain from which my prejudices flowed. Some people who had been visiting my shop for years stopped coming as a result.

Personally, I felt robbed in other ways too. The choice the commission forced upon me took away my favorite artistic outlet. It compelled me to shut down one of the most fun, challenging, and rewarding aspects of my work.

For me, creating custom wedding cakes was never mostly about making money, beyond enough to pay my staff and support my family.

I could have charged a lot more than I did for our cakes. That's not brag-ging; that's the nature of the business. People come to a custom cake designer because they want something fancy and unique, and many of them measure the artist's skill by how much he asks for his work. Ask too much, and you can price yourself out of the market. Ask too little, and people think you must not be very good at what you do.

The other thing I enjoyed most were the interactions with the happy couples—hearing how they met, what they enjoyed about each other, their dreams for the future. I liked the warmth in their conversation, the light shining in their eyes as they talked about the plans they were making together. I liked having my own small part in their special occa-sion, sharing my gifts and creativity, and forging relationships with many of them that would continue to play out as I provided other cakes for their birthdays and anniversaries and children's graduations in the years to come.

It wasn't just my business. It was my place in the community. It was my privilege to add a little delightful, tangible something to their joy and their hopes and dreams for their wedding day.

I'll never know the exact number of relationships I lost when the commission smeared my character and forced me to bow out of the wedding cake business. But I know it was a lot. For one thing, not long after the decision, I received a call from a customer who'd been coming in almost weekly for nearly twenty years. She told me she wouldn't be buying anything from me anymore. "I just can't," she said. "You're prejudiced."

That hurt.

The commissioner also opined that people of faith were primarily responsible for slavery. This was a remarkably cruel and ignorant assertion. In fact, even a cursory glance at our nation's history—indeed, world history—will show that no group was more responsible for the *abolition* of slavery than Christians, who took their cue from biblical teachings about the importance and equality of all persons in the sight of God. From William Wilberforce in England to Abraham Lincoln in the U.S., those working to end slavery grounded their efforts in humane Christian principles and the Word of God. Many of those who led the American civil rights movement, like Dr. Martin Luther King Jr., brought those same words and principles to bear on the racism of their era.

No reasonable student of history can separate the end of slavery in this country or in Europe from the advance of the Gospel and the sacrificial efforts of men and women who acted in the name of Christ and for the glory of God. To callously compare my religious convictions with those of the people who promoted slavery is more than slanderous; it's the opposite of reality.

But then, if there's one thing I've learned over these many years, it's that when reality gets in the way of an agenda, many people are more than willing to set it aside.

All of that has been painful, but nothing hurt more than one phrase the commissioner used: comparing my beliefs to those who brought on the Holocaust in World War II.

In June 1944, my dad was one of the soldiers who landed on Omaha Beach as part of "Operation Overlord"—one of three million troops under the command of General Dwight D. Eisenhower on a mission to eradicate the evil of the Nazi regime.

After landing at Normandy, my dad joined the Allied troops moving across France. He saw it all: the bombed-out towns, the stripped farmlands, the ruined lives. Widows, orphans, refugees, the wounded, the dying, the dead.

His unit struggled across France and Germany and fought in the Battle of the Bulge. This nightmarish battle came late in the war in December 1944 and January 1945 amid brutal weather conditions, including blizzards and freezing rain. Once, my dad said, he and his friends went without food for most of a week while they were limited to only six bullets per day.

Losses in this battle are almost incomprehensible: an estimated seventy-five thousand American casualties and one hundred thousand

German casualties. My dad was one of them, wounded in a mortar attack. The shrapnel left a long, jagged scar across his back, for which he later received a Purple Heart. He once told me how, while he was being transported on a jeep pulling a trailer full of other wounded soldiers, the jeep ran over a landmine, which exploded, scattering the wounded all over. They had to be loaded onto other vehicles and eventually taken to England. There, he was patched up and returned to combat, eventually moving into Germany and toward the concentration camps. ("I guess they liked my work," he said.)

But even that wasn't the worst of what my dad went through in fighting the evils of Nazism. Another horror was waiting for him: Buchenwald.

Buchenwald, in east-central Germany, is one of the most infamous camps of the entire Holocaust. About a quarter of a million prisoners—Jews, Catholics, prisoners of war, dissenters from the Nazi regime—were sent to Buchenwald, and at least fifty-five thousand perished there. Even the horrors of Normandy and the Battle of the Bulge could not prepare my dad's unit for what they found when they entered the camp. My dad did not talk much about this, but I do remember him describing how terrible the camp smelled. I've seen pictures of Buchenwald, and as I looked at the battered, emaciated bodies of the prisoners, I cannot fathom how these people were still alive, nor the cruelty of the people who could perpetrate this inhumanity.

That is how that commissioner perceived my religious beliefs. That's the kind of suffering she seems to attribute to those who ask for freedom of expression. It's a breathtakingly vicious association, utterly unfathomable—made by someone who either was utterly consumed by her own hatred or who had no sense at all of what happened in those camps. Or both.

Hearing her words—and the resounding lack of objection from the other commissioners—it was now clear to me how thoroughly the members of the commission misunderstood my beliefs and my reasons for

choosing which messages to express through my art. It was also clear
that they were deeply ignorant of a history our world cannot afford to
forget. How else to explain comparing the freedom to live out a faith that
commands us to "love your neighbor" to the calculated murder of more
than seventy-five million innocents?

It was a gross overstatement, one that insulted not only my deepest
beliefs, but also my priceless heritage and my father's legacy. Those
words cast a dark, degrading shadow over everything I'd tried to live
out in my relationships with other people and across everything I'd
wanted my business to communicate about the love of God and His
redemption story. The commissioners, in their fiery statements and in
their cold, bitter judgment, struck a painful blow against all the things
I cherish most.

They also sowed the seeds of their eventual defeat.

16

Appealing Opportunities

Our next stop was the Colorado Court of Appeals. While preparing our case for that tribunal, we filed another request for a "stay" and were again denied.

Many people will understand our choice to appeal, but some, I know, will not. "Stop poking the bear," you may be thinking. "You can't fight city hall"—much less a civil rights commission held in thrall to its own moral righteousness. All I can tell you is that I had a deepening understanding that the issues at stake were bigger than one cake artist and his little shop. This was a threat to the freedom of all Americans—to speak, or not speak...to think and believe freely...to live out their faith in the natural course of their daily lives.

When the lawyers gave me my options—cease with the ongoing legal struggle or go for the Court of Appeals—I just knew we had to reach out to the higher court.

The legal term for what the state was doing to me is "coerced speech." In my case, it means the government was trying to force me to say something I didn't want to say—or else. The "or else" for me would basically be shutting down my business by placing so many constrictions on me that I would have to choose between observing my faith or design-ing custom cakes.

Nicolle and I weren't the only ones convinced the implications of this case were getting bigger. ADF sent a staff attorney, Jeremy Tedesco, to take point on the appeal. Jeremy wasted no time communicating in public statements just how unconstitutional the commission's decisions had been up till now—and how potentially far-reaching the impact of those rulings might be.

> Every artist (he said in court) must be free to create work that
> expresses what he or she believes and not be forced to express
> contrary views. The First Amendment protects our freedom
> to speak or not speak on any issue without fear of punishment
> by the government.

That was the crux of our appeal: asking the court to reverse the com-mission's decision. The essential question was this: Does the First Amend-ment protect the free speech rights of creative professionals or not?

A second question, though, pushed its way forward during the brief months we waited for our hearing. As it turned out, David and Charlie weren't the only ones asking for custom cakes—and I wasn't the only cake artist trying to live by conscience.

About two years after my encounter with David and Charlie, a differ-ent man walked into another Denver bakery to ask for a cake that would feature two bridegrooms standing together with a big red "X" painted across them—along with some Old Testament verses condemn-ing homosexuality. He then ordered a second cake, showing Bible verses celebrating God's love for sinners, albeit with the same X-ed out picture of the two bridegrooms.

The owner of the bakery immediately declined to make either cake, saying she didn't agree with the message they presented. And, of course, I heartily agreed with her decision—I wouldn't have made those cakes either! Their message reflected an attitude toward people who identify as lesbian or gay that, to me, seemed unkind, ungracious, and unloving.

Like me, that bakery owner offered her would-be customer an alternative, just as I had in my twenty-second interaction with David and Charlie. This second owner apparently felt a similar impulse, telling the man asking for her services that she would bake him a blank cake, and provide him with the icing to paint whatever images he wanted on it.

The man rejected that offer, though, choosing instead to follow David and Charlie's example by filing a formal discrimination complaint with the Colorado Civil Rights Division against the bakery and its owner, citing the same public accommodation law.

Our cases were so similar that the second owner might well have found herself supporting my appeal, except for one thing: Neither the Colorado Civil Rights Division nor the Civil Rights Commission (on appeal) found that any discrimination had taken place. Both announced that this baker's decision to decline the orders was based on her objection to their offensive messages, not any personal prejudice against the customer. So the commissioners determined that she hadn't violated any state laws.

So how was her situation, decision, or rationale any different from mine?

They weren't.

The man who had ordered the cakes from that second Denver bakery later visited two other cake shops in town, placing essentially the same order. Those owners turned him down too, citing their objections to the message he was trying to communicate. And those owners also found themselves charged with discrimination under the same state law—and were promptly exonerated by the suddenly open-minded Civil Rights Commission.

All three of these other bakeries shared my view of our responsibility and freedom as cake designers and artists: that we should not be compelled to help communicate ideas that violate our personal beliefs. All of us were willing to serve potential customers any other items in our respective shops. Our problem was not with serving the people involved, but with creating the messages they requested.

In fact, there was only one difference between what happened in my shop and what happened in theirs—and that difference was not our professional policies or anything we said.

It was simply our point of view.

The commissioners liked the fact that all three of the other bakery owners supported same-sex marriage. And they seemingly despised the fact that I do not. So I was basically being punished for looking at the world differently than a group of unelected officials who possessed the power to put me on trial.

That blatant bias and unequal treatment became a key feature of our case going forward. Clearly, I wasn't asking for special treatment before the law. I was only asking to be treated the same way as everyone else.

The commissioners hadn't even tried to understand our argument, and they had bluntly refused to accept it. So, eventually, did the Colorado State Court of Appeals.

People have sometimes asked if I had anything to do with the man who tried to order those cakes at the other bakeries. I did not. And if by chance he'd walked into my cake shop, I wouldn't have been willing to grant his request any more than David and Charlie's.

The Court of Appeals has twenty-two judges who sit in panels (or "bancs") of three to hear cases. The three I drew determined that if helping David and Charlie say whatever they wanted forced me to violate my religious beliefs, well...my religious beliefs are collateral damage. And my First Amendment protections are too.

By that reasoning, a state could 1) compel a Democrat speechwriter to write a speech for the Republican National Convention, whether the Democrat wanted to or not; 2) force a Muslim to sing at a Christian church's Easter service; or 3) direct an LGBT web designer to create a church website promoting one-man, one-woman marriage. Or any other combination of creative expressions and belief systems.

As ridiculous as that sounds in a country grounded in the idea of personal liberty, that's the position the Court of Appeals was determined to take. And that left me with a formidable decision to make.

The immediate next step, though, was easy: We appealed to the Colorado Supreme Court. It declined to hear my case. I was surprised. I didn't know, up until this point, that the Colorado Supreme Court has discretion about which cases it accepts and which it denies. Once I realized that the Civil Rights Commission regarded my First Amendment rights as expendable and that the Court of Appeals agreed, I expected to lose at every new level of the judicial process—even at the Colorado Supreme Court.

So why go to all that effort?

Three reasons. One, of course, is that I wanted justice. I wanted to be able to create wedding cakes and continue enjoying the pleasant interactions with the couples who ordered them.

Two, my case seemed to be drawing a steadily increasing amount of attention to a government attitude that poses a profound threat to the freedom of all Americans. If I was the one—or at least one of the ones—God was using to expose this injustice, I was willing to be His instrument in that.

I told the Lord then that this was His business, His cake shop, not mine. And that whatever became of it was in His hands. I only wanted to honor Him with whatever He gave me and in whatever circumstances He placed me. And here I was. I believed it was His idea for me to be in this situation.

Which brings up the third reason. The Bible describes a moment when the prophet Daniel was in an exceedingly difficult situation: about to stand before people of authority who were not inclined to look favorably on him. He recorded what he prayed at that moment in Daniel 2:21:

And He changes the times and the seasons;
He removes kings and raises up kings.... (emphasis mine)

Like Daniel, I believe that the times and the seasons, as well as the power and authority of "kings," are in God's hands. If courts were to rule against me, so be it. My fate and my future, and those of the people I love most, are in His hands. So I will never have anything to fear from pressing forward.

By mid-2016, after four years of litigation and nothing but losses to show for it, "pressing forward" only allowed for one last option: an appeal to the U.S. Supreme Court.

17

Trying for the Supreme Court

o say that appealing your case to the U.S. Supreme Court is a "long shot" is really an understatement—a pretty big understatement. Let me explain just how big.

The high court is usually asked to hear about eight to ten thousand cases per year. In the end, it usually agrees to rule on seventy or eighty of them. That's less than 1 percent. And, of course, if the Supreme Court says no, the lower court's ruling stands.

Just to illustrate this, I put together a little demonstration for my family. I put ten thousand chocolate chips in a container to represent all the applications the court receives. Then I stirred in eighty vanilla chips to represent the handful of cases the court accepts. Finally, I stirred in one strawberry chip, to represent *Masterpiece Cakeshop v. Colorado Civil Rights Commission*.

For my case to be heard, the justices would have to sift through and thoroughly examine all those chocolate and vanilla chips and deliberately take out the red one. Then at least four justices would have to agree that the red one is worthy of the court's time and attention. So each of the four would have to purposefully pull that one red chip out from among all the chocolates and vanillas.

Those are long odds.

In my case, a couple of other considerations made the odds even longer.

For one thing, it had not risen through the legal system in the usual way. Normally, a case like mine would have been heard at the state supreme court. Because Colorado's had declined my case, the U.S. Supreme Court allowed a last-chance appeal—although the chances of it agreeing to hear one of these out-of-nowhere cases are very slim.

That's because the U.S. Supreme Court prefers to rule as a kind of tiebreaker in cases where different state supreme courts or federal appellate courts have issued conflicting decisions. The latter is called a "circuit split," and in such cases the high court will often step in to settle the contradiction, lest the issue at stake spread confusion throughout the nation's legal system. The First Amendment, for instance, can't mean one thing in the Ninth Circuit and something else in the Seventh.

As my case presented relatively new issues, there would likely be no great sense of urgency, from the justices' point of view, to settle the issues my case raised. Indeed, they had already passed on similar cases in recent years. So we would need to find some way to impress a sense of urgency on at least four members of the Supreme Court.

One way to do that would be to persuade the justices that an issue of significant national or historical importance was at stake. Something with a bearing on the constitutional freedoms of millions of Americans.

A second way might be to convince the Supreme Court that—even if the issues at stake had not yet prompted a full-blown "circuit split"— there was enough growing confusion and disagreement to call for a decisive assessment.

A third option would be to demonstrate that the Supreme Court itself has not been entirely consistent in its rulings related to a given issue and that the time has come for a "once-and-for-all" ruling to settle the lingering questions.

And then there's always the fourth and perhaps most reliable approach: appeal to the justices' hearts. Tell them a human story that engages their emotions as well as their legal intellect and persuade them that this painful situation can only be resolved through their unique intervention.

Any of those approaches can make the crucial difference in whether a case is granted a hearing or not; the more of those four aspects an attorney can bring to bear on any given case, I'm told, the better.

My attorneys were convinced that most of these criteria applied. We could clearly demonstrate that the lower courts' rulings posed a serious threat to a multitude of Americans' First Amendment protections—particularly as applied to the free-speech rights of creative artists and the religious freedom of those who believe marriage is a union between one man and one woman.

ADF attorneys were representing several artists in these kinds of cases. One was Barronelle Stutzman, a floral artist in Washington state who had declined a request from a friend (and favorite customer of nearly ten years) to design creative floral art for his same-sex wedding. Another was Blaine Adamson, owner of a Kentucky printing company, who had declined to print custom T-shirts for an LGBT pride festival.

Those cases were in various stages of litigation, as were a half dozen others raising similar questions, primarily: Can the government force an artist to communicate a message he or she disagrees with or one that goes against that artist's sincere religious beliefs?

We could only hope the Supreme Court would find my story compelling. Not only was my state government clearly trying to compel my speech, but there also was the double standard applied by the lower courts, the blatant antagonism toward my faith, and the emotional and financial impact the unjust rulings had had on my life, my business, and my family to take into account. We hoped the justices would discern that for too many Colorado officials, destroying me had become a personal cause—that they were, in effect, "after me."

I assumed the worst that could happen would be that the Supreme Court might deny my petition. But as one of my attorneys pointed out, that was not the worst possibility.

On the one hand, he said, if the court denied my request—and the lower courts' rulings stood—I would not only be out of the wedding-cake business, but possibly out of the cake-design business, period. The courts' decisions opened the door for anyone to walk in and demand a message I couldn't in good conscience accommodate. And I would have little choice but to comply, unless I stopped my creative expressions altogether. Without the cake designs, I probably wouldn't have enough business to keep the shop open—or to employ my daughter Lisa, a single parent who not only has her own remarkable talent for cake design, but also treasures the shop's safe setting that allows her to work while homeschooling her children.

All of that could go away quickly if the U.S. Supreme Court simply turned us down.

But on the other hand, my attorney reminded me, the justices could agree to hear my case—and then rule against me. If that happened, not only would all the things I just mentioned probably happen, but millions upon millions of my fellow Americans would see some of their most precious freedoms compromised and have to live with their own consequences of the court's decision.

So no pressure.

My ADF attorneys were willing to do all the hard, painstaking work required to complete the legal paperwork and put my petition before the justices. But the final decision of whether to petition the highest court in America was up to me.

During those discussions, I recalled a scene from a movie I'd seen years before, *Facing the Giants*. In it, a father talks with his discouraged son about the boy's fears of trying out for his new school's football team. The boy is a soccer player, but his school only offers football—limiting his outlet for athletic expression.

"Why not try out for the football team?" the dad asks.

"They've already got a good kicker," the son replies. "What if I don't even make the team?"

"Well, you're already not on the team," the dad says. "I mean, you can't get any more 'not on the team' than you are right now."

I thought about those lines as we considered the odds of having the U.S. Supreme Court consider our case:

"What if they deny us? We'll never be heard."

"You're already not being heard. You can't be any more 'not heard' than you already are."

"So the worst that can happen is that the court denies our petition, and then we're *officially* not heard."

"No, the worst that can happen is that the court grants your petition, you are heard, and you lose."

The last realization was stunning. I finally understood that this case was about the freedom of all Americans, not one simple man in a small cake shop.

I got it.

I wanted my actions to follow my faith. And I wasn't willing to accept defeat. All those earlier losses, I knew, were ultimately just the legal stepping stones necessary to bring us to this.

On July 22, 2016, we petitioned the U.S. Supreme Court to hear the case of *Masterpiece Cakeshop v. Colorado Civil Rights Commission.*

18

Media Blitz

I t would be nearly a year before the high court announced whether it had agreed to hear my case. That's an unusually long stretch. The first time the justices conferenced was September 26, 2016. They finally granted certiorari on June 26, 2017. Our case was relisted a record eighteen times—meaning that the justices actually talked about the merits of my case in their private meetings that many times.

A little background on how the justices come to their decisions: An appeal to a higher court is referred to as a writ of certiorari. (That's Latin for "a request to be made certain.") It's a formal legal request for one judicial body to review the decision of a lower court. Sometimes it's called a "cert petition" for short. And when the higher court agrees to do so, that's called "granting cert."

As I mentioned, at least four justices have to agree to hear a case before cert is granted. The building of that four-justice consensus usually takes place "in conference." The nine judges go into a room by themselves and close the doors. There they talk, reason, argue, and debate the relative merits of hearing a particular case with each other. When they emerge, they bring with them one of four announcements regarding each case that's been pitched to them:

They can deny cert—"We decline to hear this case."

They can grant cert—"We agree to hear this case."

They can re-conference the case—"We didn't get to this one yet." (There's still hope.)

Or they can relist the case—"We talked about it, but we haven't made up our minds on it yet." (More hope—it's likely that at least one justice is championing this case but hasn't managed to talk three others into coming on board.)

As I mentioned, my case was re-conferenced eighteen times. That means that for whatever reason, the justices weren't ready to hear it—but weren't of a mind to dismiss it either. It's possible that since Justice Antonin Scalia had passed away the previous February, they wanted to wait to take the case until after his replacement had been appointed and confirmed. We know they first put it on the list when the fall session began in September 2016 (just two months after we filed our petition). But they didn't render a final decision until June 2017, when they were on their way out the door for their summer vacations.

That means *Masterpiece* sat on their to-do list for literally the entire Supreme Court term.

Whatever the reasons for that delay, their decision was more than worth waiting for. On June 26, the justices granted cert in *Masterpiece Cakeshop v. Colorado Civil Rights Commission.*

That was a Monday, and I was in the shop early, as usual. It was the last day of the term for the high court, so I expected this might be the day. As had become my habit, I paused amid my morning getting-ready-to-open activities and checked an online resource, SCO-TUSblog, to see what announcements the court might have issued.

And there were the five words we'd been waiting and praying to receive: "*Masterpiece Cakeshop* has been granted."

I was too overcome to actually call anyone. I tried, but my voice kept cracking, and I choked up every time I tried to talk. So I quickly sent a few happy texts to Debi and the family. No one else was around, except for a homeless guy who sometimes comes into the shop early for coffee.

Grinning ear to ear, I leaned across my desk and said to him, "Hey— I'm going to the Supreme Court!"

He looked over at me, not especially impressed.

"Yeah," he said, "I gotta go to court on Wednesday."

With our court date set for December 5, things began moving fast. The next few hours were a blur of friends and family calling or coming by—or both—to hug and laugh and just share in the general rejoicing. Against all those long, long odds, we were in.

And ADF called. I was scheduled to appear on one of the network morning talk shows in New York the next day. I had to run for the airport to catch the first flight out.

That was the start of another blur of activity—four crowded months of interviews, travel, events, personal appearances, and ongoing consultations with my attorneys. My case drew a great deal of media attention as journalists jockeyed to figure out how the high court would rule.

I mentioned in earlier chapters some of my first experiences talking to reporters. I was grateful that God had helped me say the right words and that, often, I had been able to stay pretty much on message in those interviews, accurately explaining what I had done and said and why. But this, my attorneys warned me, was no time to get overconfident in my communication skills. Anyone who's watched much television news can see that the best reporters are adept at getting people to say what the media outlets want them to say, rather than what the people themselves had hoped to communicate.

As my case had moved up the legal ladder, ADF had brought me and my attorneys in to help me tell my story and communicate more consistently what I wanted people to understand about my case. That takes a particular kind of discipline, because most of us are easily distracted by an unexpected question, and few of us are used to explaining ourselves in the very limited space of a five- to ten-second soundbite.

It took me a while to get the hang of it, but my sister Trish took it upon herself to put me through my paces, asking me questions and critiquing my answers whenever there was a lull in the work of the shop. Actually, customers themselves inadvertently gave me a lot of good practice, since many of them had heard of my case and often asked me about what had happened and why I was doing what I was doing.

By this point, ADF had paired me with a new lead attorney, Kristen Waggoner, who would argue my case before the Supreme Court. We made countless appearances together on TV and radio in the months before she presented our arguments at the court, and she proved consistently good at keeping both of us to the straight and narrow of messaging whenever we were on the air.

One of my biggest tests came within days of the court's announcement that it had granted our cert petition. Kristen and I were invited to appear on *The View*—a national talk show I was not familiar with (I don't watch TV), but my attorneys assured me it would draw a large audience, particularly of women, and put me up close with a group of outspoken ladies who likely would not be especially friendly to my point of view. Our goal was to help viewers understand why my case mattered to all Americans, regardless of how they might feel about same-sex marriage.

Joy Behar would be hosting a panel that included Paula Faris, Jedediah Bila, Sara Haines, and Sunny Hostin. The ADF media team studied the show closely in the days before our appearance there and put together a list of questions they thought the various women would be likely to ask. In fact, their predictions turned out to be uncannily accurate.

People sometimes ask me what the women of *The View* were like; I don't really know—it's not as though we went to lunch after the show. What you see on the screen is pretty much what I saw on the set, except that I had a good view of the audience too. Assistants walked us out on stage during a commercial break. We took our seats while the women studied their questions for the coming segment, written on little blue cards. After commercials, the audiences at home and in the studio saw a video giving the background of my case. Then the director pointed at a camera, and away we went.

Most of the women were gracious in their hellos and goodbyes, and in between, the questions and commentary ran the gamut from Ms. Behar's "Wouldn't Jesus bake the cake?" to Ms. Hostin's "When I put my legal hat on" (she's an attorney) "I think [this issue] is a closer call than we're giving credit for." I answered their questions as best I could, spoke up when they asked me to (even wearing a microphone, I'm a pretty soft-spoken guy), and tried to communicate the importance of my faith and the reality of my love for others, including David and Charlie.

I was glad Kristen was there to do the heavy lifting of explaining the law and of underscoring the fact that millions of people around the world, from many different religious persuasions, share my beliefs on same-sex marriage.

Another particularly memorable interview was a guest appearance on the *Megyn Kelly Today* show. Once again, we'd practiced hard to anticipate what Ms. Kelly might ask and how best to respond. Once again, we wanted to dispel incorrect information in the media and help people understand what was at stake.

We were still backstage, ready to go on the air, when Ms. Kelly herself looked in to tell us that because David and Charlie had decided not to appear on the show, she felt duty-bound to speak from their point of view. So I understood she would not be making any extra effort to appear neutral during our interview.

"This could be tougher than we even expected," Kristen cautioned me as we prepared to go out on stage. And indeed, it seemed at first to be going that way. But thankfully, I was able to stay on message, to keep my replies clear and concise—and even to catch Ms. Kelly herself off-guard with my reply to one of her questions.

She had asked what kinds of cakes I would decline to make, and I mentioned that, among many others, I wouldn't create a cake that spoke unkindly of LGBT individuals.

She seemed stunned.

"People would ask you for a cake that disparaged LGBT?"

"Yes, they have."

"People want cakes that discriminate against gay people?" She couldn't get over it.

"Yes," I said, "and I've turned those down, as well—because it's another message that I can't create." It was an unexpected opportunity to make especially clear that I don't hate anyone, and that my position stems solely from concerns about creating a message I don't agree with.

My attorneys estimate that I did hundreds of those kinds of interviews—with newspapers including the *Washington Post*, the *Los Angeles Times*, the *Denver Post*, the *Seattle Times*, the *Wall Street Journal*, and the *New York Times*; on radio with hosts like Peter Boyles, Eric Metaxas, Ben Shapiro, Dennis Prager, Todd Starnes, Glenn Beck, Focus on the Family president Jim Daly, and James Dobson of *Family Talk*; and on television with Fox News journalists like Harris Faulkner, Laura Ingraham, and Shannon Bream, the panel at *Fox & Friends*, and others, as well as reporters for *Nightline*, *The Today Show*, ABC, CNN, and CBN News.

Add to that list appearances at various conservative and Christian gatherings, giving short speeches, being interviewed on stage, or answering questions from the audience, and you can begin to imagine how the travel time piled up in those months before our hearing at the Supreme Court—then afterward while we awaited our decision, and finally in the wake of the court's June ruling. Thankfully, I always had an ADF attorney by my side.

After a while, a lot of these appearances began to blur together, and since I'm not one to watch myself on camera, I've never even seen most of those recordings. A few I remember for the grace of the interviewer (Ms. Faulkner of Fox News was particularly kind), or for feeling afterward that I had communicated my position a little more clearly than usual, or that I had at least figured out what to do with my hands.

We didn't agree to any of those media opportunities to raise money or to make me famous. We just wanted people to understand my case, who I was, that I genuinely cared about all people, that I sincerely wanted to honor God in my business, and that our Constitution protects my right to live out my faith and decide for myself what messages I will and will not communicate.

Sometimes, even today, customers will walk into the cake shop with no idea who I am or how much media coverage our little business has stirred up over the years. I'll be wrapping up some cookies or brownies, and then I'll hear them say, "Heyyyy…I know who you are." Or, "I saw you on [insert TV news show]." It's funny that after all those flights and airports and green rooms and soundstages and banquet halls, so many strangers remember my moments in the spotlight better than I do.

19

At the Supreme Court

December 2017 drew near, and with it the date for our hearing before the Supreme Court.

On the Sunday before the arguments, our pastor invited me and Debi up to the front of the congregation at the close of the morning service. He wanted to pray for us, and he asked our fellow church members to join him in doing so.

"You may or may not agree with the stand Jack is taking," he said. "But this is the U.S. Supreme Court. This impacts the whole country. This is very important." And with that, he asked God's blessing on our trip to D.C., our family and attorneys, the arguments, and whatever came of our time in the courtroom.

He wasn't the only one to recognize the significance of this case. About fifty amicus (friend-of-the-court) briefs had been filed by those on each side of the issue who were not directly involved in the case.

That number of briefs indicated a broad sensibility within legal circles that this case had serious implications for both the law and the culture. A lot of people were going to be converging on Washington, D.C., that week. Some would be holding the ever-present microphones and cameras, hungry to capture every image and soundbite of the event for history. Some would be offering their exclusive perspective and commentary for the major papers, radio broadcasts, and TV news programs. Many would be holding placards and bullhorns, crowding together to cheer and jeer outside the court itself.

A high-profile Supreme Court case—even outside the high marble walls of the Court itself—is a three-ring circus of media, pop culture, and the law.

I didn't realize most of that until later. Sunday afternoon, I was just trying to get myself and my family to the airport. Lisa would be joining me, and Debi and would bring with her three of our grandchildren. My sisters, Trish and Linda, would be coming too, along with their husbands. My older daughter, Jennifer, would be traveling from her home in Montreal to join us in D.C.

On the door of the shop, I hung a sign: "Will be closed this week. Going to Washington, D.C. for the Supreme Court of the United States. Will open again on December 11." It was the first time I'd closed the shop that long since I'd opened it nearly twenty-five years earlier.

We arrived in D.C. Sunday evening, went straight to the hotel, then out for a late dinner with the legal team preparing my case. Monday, Kristen Waggoner and another ADF attorney, Jim Campbell, huddled over the arguments she'd be making Tuesday morning, while I had an hour or two to play tourist with my wife and family before heading back to the hotel to hunker down with the ADF media team, working through my remarks and responses for after the hearing.

That evening, we ate dinner at the hotel. ADF president Mike Farris came by later to join several of us in a time of prayer for the events to come, and in particular for Kristen, as she presented our arguments to the court. And then we headed to our rooms, where we all tried, with mixed success, to sleep and settle our minds and hearts for the next day.

December in Washington is cold, but that Tuesday was not too bad. It was a gray day, but nearly sixty degrees, with a light breeze keeping a nip in the air. Debi, who tends to be more anxious than I do, actually woke up calm, at peace, and ready to go. That was a great encouragement to me. We gathered the family, grabbed some breakfast, and by 8:00 a.m. we were on our way to the court.

My original attorneys, Nicolle Martin and Jeremy Tedesco, joined us to lead our way into the building. Also with us was Barronelle Stutzman, who had become a dear friend of mine as we grew to know her and her husband, Darold, at various ADF events. Barronelle is the floral artist from Richland, Washington—a warm, gracious, soft-spoken woman whose case in many ways mirrors mine. It was eventually heard at the Washington Supreme Court—but since Colorado's had turned mine down, our case leapfrogged over hers to arrive at the at the U.S. Supreme Court first.

If you haven't visited Washington, D.C., or been to the U.S. Supreme Court, you might not realize that the front of the building is directly across the street from the U.S. Capitol. In fact, the front steps of the court face the back steps of the Capitol. It's an impressive setting; you realize you're stepping out of your car and into the epicenter of American government, surrounded in every direction by centuries of extraordinary history.

Before I could even lift my eyes to those magnificent marble columns, my vision was drawn to the fast-growing crowd swarming the sidewalks in front of the court. I really wasn't prepared for the hundreds of people there—some waving signs, some already chanting their slogans. David and Charlie on one hand, and me on the other, seemed to have drawn our respective share of enthusiasts, though I was honored to see how many had graciously come out to support me.

Several ADF team members and supporters stood in the line for the courtroom. Our attorneys reminded me that only about seventy people are allowed to sit in the courtroom to hear oral arguments—and the rule is first come, first seated. I learned that people had actually been lining up on the sidewalk for five days, eating out of coolers, enduring the very cold nights bundled up in sleeping bags on the sidewalk, taking turns running to nearby restaurants for a bathroom, passing the time playing cards and checking cellphones.

It was loud out there on the sidewalk—so loud I really couldn't make out much of what anyone was saying as we followed Jeremy toward our designated entrance. I did manage to make out what was printed on some of the placards dancing in a sea of signs:

It's Not About the Cake, Jack

Tolerance Is a Two-Way Street

Free the Cake Baker

ACLU: Open to All

Jack Phillips Serves All People But Can't Create All Art (That was a crowded sign.)

Justice for Jack

We Got Your Back, Jack

Et cetera. It was especially good to see that (as was the case with the chants) the signs and messages supporting us appeared more numerous and prominent than those opposing us—and also that the shouts of hope and encouragement mostly drowned out the obscenities. Some harsh words cut the morning air, many of them clearly aimed at me. But they didn't rattle me. By then, I'd heard and seen pretty much everything, usually from a voice yelling in my ear over the phone or hateful words glaring up at me from an email.

High above me, in tall letters carved in the beautiful white stone above the great pillars at the main entrance of the court, were the words "Equal Justice Under Law." That's all I'd ever wanted or asked for. Not special privilege in honor of my faith. Not official, sanctioned agreement with my personal point of view. Not some mighty pronouncement that I was right and everyone else was wrong.

Simply a fair hearing before a fair court. A ruling that honored the abiding truths of our Constitution. And, I prayed, an affirmation of two particular truths that we as Americans have for so long held to be (as our Declaration of Independence says) "self-evident": freedom of speech and free exercise of our religious liberty.

Our God-given right as individuals to speak, or not speak, in accordance with the certainties of our heart. And our right to believe to the depths of our soul and to conscientiously act on those beliefs.

That was what had brought me down the long, winding path of my life and my case—not a desire to spar with angry people or be dragged into a shouting match, but simply to see those enduring truths affirmed. To hear one of the most crucial decisions of my life defended by my attorney, my friend. To seek justice, confident that the outcome was firmly in God's hands.

D ebi and I followed Jeremy and Nicolle up the steps and around to an entryway on the south side of the western façade. As we moved past the guards and through the door, the noise from the sidewalk faded, and Debi gave me a relieved half-smile. Perhaps someday all the tumult that had engulfed us these last few years would subside, and we'd be living in peace and something like happy anonymity again.

We moved through security, one of the last clear vestiges of the twenty-first century, as we passed up a flight of stairs to immerse ourselves for a while in history. The halls of the court are saturated with an ambience of dignity and quiet seriousness—a place where great business is done. The branching hallways are lined with portraits of some of the more famous justices, while the Great Hall has alcoves on each side featuring marble busts of every chief justice since John Jay began serving in 1789.

(Jay, by the way, had an interesting view on government—one that those who oppose my legal case may not fully appreciate. "No human society," he said, "has ever been able to maintain both order and freedom, both cohesiveness and liberty apart from the moral precepts of the Christian religion...should our Republic ever forget this fundamental precept of governance...this great experiment will then be surely doomed." Amen.)

We joined the small crowd milling about in the Great Hall outside the actual courtroom. I immediately began looking about for Art Lien, the renowned artist primarily responsible for rendering what goes on in the court, where cameras are not allowed. I greatly admire his work and follow it on SCOTUSblog.com. I had been hoping for the chance to make his acquaintance and express my admiration. Unfortunately, he was out that day, and some other artist would be making the sketches in his stead.

I became aware of hushed voices and pointed fingers—some aimed at me, some at David and Charlie, who were also in the group waiting to go into the courtroom.

At 9:00 a.m. sharp, the doors of the courtroom opened, and we all lined up to walk through a second security screening, complete with metal detectors. Security is unusually (if understandably) strict at the court, and no one is allowed to carry anything into the main courtroom but a pen and some paper. No cameras or tape recorders are allowed; reporters in the court take their notes the old-fashioned way. Also no phones, no keys, no loose change—nothing with the potential to make inappropriate noise or disrupt the formal proceedings. Small lockers are provided for those who have come full-pocketed and unprepared.

Once past the detectors, we mounted two short steps, passed one more security guard, and moved into the courtroom.

As a longtime, informal student of architecture, all of Washington, D.C., holds a wonderful fascination for me, and of course, the interior of our highest court is no exception. The main room seems a little smaller than you might expect (eighty-two by ninety-one feet), but the ceiling is forty-four feet high. Twenty-four columns hewn from Italian marble are spaced along all sides of the room. The walls and ceiling are made of Spanish marble. High, thick red curtains line all sides of the room as well, and along the top of the north and south walls are two ivory friezes: the one on the south highlights famous lawgivers of the ancient world (including Moses and Solomon), while the one on the north features prominent lawgivers from the Middle Ages to the present (including Charlemagne, Sir William Blackstone, and John Marshall).

Along the front of the room is a wing-shaped, elevated bench of dark mahogany with high-backed, fine-leathered office chairs for the justices. To the left of that bench is a desk where the clerk of the court sits; this person is responsible for the court's docket, calendar, and special activities. A little farther to that side, on red benches, sit members of the press, listening and scribbling their notes.

To the right of the bench sits the marshal of the court, who's responsible for security (the court has its own police force) and for keeping time and signaling the attorneys when their allotted minutes for argument begin and end. A little farther to that side are some other red benches where guests of the justices are permitted to sit. Officers of the court and important visitors sit on black chairs placed in front of the special guests.

The attorneys presenting arguments sit at tables facing the bench. Between the tables is a lectern, where they stand to make their statements and answer questions from the justices. Behind them stretches a bronze railing separating them from the onlookers. The court itself has room for 250 observers, with 125 wooden chairs on each side of a broad aisle. The floor has red carpet, the ceiling is ornamented, and everything is clean, dignified, and polished within an inch of its life.

We made our way to our seats, and I quickly discovered that the federal marshals who supervise the seating are sticklers about "first come, first seated." You file in, and you take what you get. (It's a little like musical chairs, when the music stops.) No moving for a better angle, no trading seats with your friend—you sit where you sit, and you stay there.

We sat down—Jeremy, Nicolle, myself, and Debi in one row, with Lisa, Trish, and Barronelle behind us. I noticed David, Charlie, and Charlie's mother sitting off to our right. Along with the neat rows of seats, I saw more wooden chairs along the walls and at the back of the room. The court was expecting a bigger-than-usual crowd today. Instinctively, I began calculating our place in the filling courtroom and realized that my seat—three rows back from the front, three seats in on the right side of the aisle—was situated in the exact center of the room. *Appropriate enough,* I thought ruefully, given that I'd been in the middle of all of this for five and a half years.

One of our group raised a hand to point out some feature of the room to the others; a marshal immediately directed us to keep our hands down. As the room filled up and the general hubbub grew, other marshals demanded that everyone lower their voices: "It will be quiet in here!" The room fell silent, then the noise slowly grew like a rising tide, and the marshal had to shush us again. "It WILL be quiet in here!" he barked. And it was again—for a few more minutes.

I glanced again at David and Charlie, wondering if their thoughts were running along the same path as mine. Everyone else in the room either had an official role in the legal system or was a spectator watching the show. Although our case had far-reaching implications—otherwise none of us would be there at all—we and our loved ones knew what it was like to be at the eye of this legal hurricane all this time and what this kind of closure would mean for us individually heading forward.

An hour later, the room was full, and the marshals were still trying to keep the murmuring to a minimum. The reporters up front were whispering with each other. Kristen and Jim came in, taking their seats at one of the tables facing the bench. Along with their briefcases, Jim was carrying a box of files with every detail of information on the case, ready to retrieve any pertinent facts Kristen might need at a moment's notice.

This was Kristen's first argument before the U.S. Supreme Court. She'd been preparing intensively for months, working with Jim and Jeremy and others from ADF to craft her statements and steel herself for every conceivable question the justices might ask. Our preparation for the ladies of *The View* was nothing compared to what went into getting ready for these jurists.

Kristen had already undergone several "moot courts" in which a panel of her ADF peers and other respected legal professionals acted out trial runs of what she might expect at the high court, firing questions the justices were likely to pose and trying to catch her off-guard with penetrating arguments of their own, designed to poke holes at any weak point in our case.

It was strenuous work, to say the least, and though she never showed it, I knew she was likely as tired as she was focused, coming into that courtroom. She'd been immersed in everything Masterpiece for months... and the moment of truth was finally at hand.

Sitting at the adjoining table was ACLU attorney David Cole, representing David and Charlie. Undoubtedly, they had their own considerable pressures to deal with. Seated nearby was Colorado Solicitor General Frederick Yarger, who was there to argue on behalf of the Civil Rights Commission and how it had handled my case. Also at hand was U.S. Solicitor General Noel Francisco, who would present the federal government's view on all of this—which, happily, supported my position.

Like most people, I didn't understand many of the unique aspects of arguing at the Supreme Court. For one thing, the attorneys never face the crowd or each other—they present only to the nine justices. Nor are any witnesses called at this rarified level of jurisprudence. The justices have already read the arguments in the briefs provided by the parties involved; they've also read (or had their clerks read) those amicus briefs I mentioned earlier. They know the facts and the arguments for both sides. Technically, they don't really need any more information to make up their minds and issue a ruling. (Indeed, one of the justices, Clarence Thomas, almost always declines to actively participate in the breakneck Q&A that so frequently erupts at these hearings. When my case was heard, he had gone more than ten years without asking a question in oral arguments. He didn't ask any in mine either.)

Still, this marked the justices' one opportunity to question each party's attorney face to face. At the time, the justices could commence questioning from the moment an attorney steps up to the lectern. Given that each party is given only half an hour to present its arguments, the justices often waste no time firing off their questions. That's especially true in a case like mine, where the underlying issues are highly charged, and the implications of the ruling could have a particularly broad impact on the nation's laws and culture. (After my case, the court made a new rule, giving each attorney a full two minutes for an opening statement before receiving any questions.)

The court, of course, would not issue an opinion that day. The justices would convene later to debate the arguments and relative merits of each party's position, then issue an opinion later—likely in late spring or early summer, near the close of the current session. The court frequently saves decisions on its most volatile and controversial cases for late in the term.

It was almost time. I felt Debi slip her hand into mine. It was a sobering moment. We were half relieved to finally be here, to see our questions settled once and for all—and half on edge with suspense, knowing that whatever this court determined would be final. No more appeals after this. Nowhere to go from here.

The judicial branch is responsible for one third of our nation's government activities. The Supreme Court is the towering pinnacle of that division. All we'd been through the last few years had built to this. As the court marshal rose and lifted his gavel, we took a deep breath.

It was all in the Lord's hands now. As it always had been.

20

Oral Arguments

The gavel came down. A door opened behind the bench, the red curtains were swept aside, and the nine justices filed into the room, taking their seats with barely a glance toward the waiting audience.

The justices sit in order of seniority: Chief Justice John Roberts at the center, the longest-serving justice to his right, the second-longest-serving to his left, and back and forth, in that order. Neil Gorsuch, then the most newly appointed of the nine, sat on the far-left end.

Across the rest of the bench sat Associate Justices Ruth Bader Ginsburg, Stephen Breyer, Samuel Alito, Sonia Sotomayor, Elena Kagan, Anthony Kennedy, and Clarence Thomas. A formidable array of remarkable legal minds. How would they choose to look on my case?

We were about to find out.

The court marshal let forth the words he uses to open every session of the U.S. Supreme Court:

"The Honorable, the Chief Justice and the Associate Justices of the Supreme Court of the United States. Oyez! Oyez! Oyez! All persons having business before the Honorable, the Supreme Court of the United States, are admonished to draw near and give their attention, for the Court is now sitting. God save the United States and this Honorable Court!"

And with that, we were off to the races.

R oberts got right to the point. "We'll hear argument this morning in Case 16-111, *Masterpiece Cakeshop versus Colorado Civil Rights Commission*. Ms. Waggoner."

Kristen stepped up to the podium.

"Mr. Chief Justice, and may it please the Court," she began. "The First Amendment prohibits the government from forcing people to express messages that violate their religious convictions. Yet the commission orders Mr. Phillips to do just that."

And that, of course, was our entire argument in a nutshell: that I shouldn't be forced to design and create custom cakes that celebrate same-sex marriage when I believe the Bible defines marriage as between one man and one woman.

It was a good thing that Kristen got such a clear, concise summary of our argument out of the way so quickly. Before she could utter another word, the justices hit her with a barrage of questions.

She was facing what attorneys like to call a "hot bench." The justices' questions tumbled over each other as they leaned into their microphones, interrupting, raising their voices, jockeying for their place in the interrogation queue. Only Justice Thomas sat apart from all this, leaning back in his chair, watching and maintaining his customary silence.

At moments, it felt more like a middle school dodgeball game than the dignified atmosphere of the nation's highest court. Kristen hardly had time to breathe, let alone finish her opening statement. But she rose wonderfully to the challenge. She fielded the rapid-fire questions coming in from all directs with poise and a level tone. She was quick, accurate, compelling, and—I thought—convincing.

I realized, not for the first time, that I had a very good lawyer.

She and the other attorneys had told me to be listening for one particular question that they expected the justices not only to ask but to press especially hard: In my case, does a custom cake designed to celebrate marriage constitute "speech"?

They were right. That turned out to be exactly the question on many of the justices' minds. Ginsburg wanted to know whether anyone could buy a cake off my shelf. When Kristen said yes, Kennedy wondered whether that kind of cake constituted speech.

Ginsburg still wanted clarity about who I'd sell to and what I'd sell. "You're not challenging his obligation to sell his ordinary wares, his already-made wares?" she asked.

"Not at all," Kristen said. "Mr. Phillips offered the couple anything in his store, as well as offered to sell additional cakes, custom cakes, that would express other messages." I was really glad she had a chance to explain that specific point, because it was such an important part of the case for me. It really defined my culture of welcome. I wanted the justices—and all the Americans who would read about these arguments—to understand I welcomed everybody into my shop.

Ginsburg followed with yet another question. "At a wedding ceremony, I take it, the speech is of the people who are marrying and perhaps the officiant, but…who else speaks at a wedding?"

"The artists speak, Justice Ginsburg," said Kristen. "It's as much Mr. Phillips's speech as it would be the couple's." She was trying to make it clear that my custom cakes remain my speech even when someone pays me to create them.

From there the questions started running even faster in every direction.

But that one key question kept coming up again and again, in one form or another—what is speech? Can a custom cake (or any other work of art, architecture, or design) be protected under the heading of "free speech"—that is, the First Amendment?

"Certainly not all cakes would be considered speech," Kristen said, "but in the wedding context, Mr. Phillips is painting on a blank canvas. He is creating a painting on that canvas that expresses messages, including words and symbols in those messages."

At one point, a question directed at Kristen caused Lisa to wince. Barronelle instinctively reached out to put a comforting arm around her shoulder. Immediately, the nearest federal marshal leaned over and half-hissed, half-whispered, "You will put your hands down and in front of you!" Barronelle yanked back her arm. After that, I'm pretty sure they both sat rigidly with their hands solemnly in their laps for the rest of the argument!

That little reprimand underscored the gravity of the situation for all of us. But Kristen never knew it happened. She just kept answering the downpour of questions, which showed no sign of slacking off.

In the last few seconds allotted to her, Kristen was able to close with one more brief statement about not forcing someone to express messages or create a piece of art they don't believe in. "They believe that they can compel the speech of filmmakers, oil painters, and graphic designers in all kinds of contexts." And with that, a red light lit up on the court marshal's desk, indicating that she had reached the end of the time allowed for her opening argument.

Roberts said, "We'll afford you the full rebuttal time." Kristen thanked him, and with a silent prayer, I'm sure, thanked the Lord as well. The justices had consumed virtually all of her time with questions, and recognizing that, Roberts used his discretion to give her a little more opportunity to present her own arguments. It was a generous gift. While not unprecedented, it certainly wasn't routine—but then, very little about this case could be deemed "routine."

I, too, was thankful for the extra time and thought it was another sign of God's hand on all these circumstances. Kristen had done an amazing job responding to the many questions that had come her way, but I also knew she still had more crucial arguments to make.

The time came for the federal government to share its position. That task fell to Solicitor General Noel Francisco.

The solicitor general is essentially the attorney who argues for the U.S. government at the U.S. Supreme Court. It's his job to monitor cases coming before the court and determine any in which the federal government seems to have a special interest. He then files an amicus brief on behalf of whichever party he thinks best, and usually requests time during oral arguments to present the government's own points of support for that side.

That request is no small thing, because time is an exceedingly precious commodity at the high court. If the solicitor general asks for an opportunity to speak, his time is deducted from that of the attorney he is supporting—which was only thirty minutes to start with.

In this instance, the court gave Kristen twenty minutes and Francisco ten. Having the federal government arguing on your behalf is a wonderful thing, but ten minutes is a lot of time to give up when you have as many points as Kristen had left to make. That's why Roberts's gift of extra minutes was so deeply appreciated.

The federal government's primary concern with my case involved the principle of freedom of speech.

Ginsburg obliged that concern by launching the discussion with questions about the Free Speech Clause. "How narrow is it? We've got the answer that the florist is in the same place as the cake maker; so is the person who designs the invitations and the menus. I don't see a line that can be drawn..."

Before Francisco could reply, Kennedy chimed in. "But the problem...is that so many of these examples do involve free speech...if you prevail, could the baker put a sign in his window, 'We do not bake cakes for gay weddings'?"

"Your Honor," Francisco said, "I think that the baker could say he does not make custom-made wedding cakes for gay weddings, but most cakes would not cross that threshold..."

My mind was spinning, trying to follow the legal arguments in this increasingly fast-paced tennis match between attorney and justices. I was having a hard time guessing where the discussion was going.

Kagan and Sotomayor jumped in, leading the solicitor general through more examples and discussion: chefs and florists, weddings and other ceremonies. Francisco held fast to his point that, with an

event like a wedding, some form of speech was inevitably involved—
and no artist should be forced to invest their personal creativity in a
ceremony they opposed.

That I understood, and this felt like solid legal ground to me.

Then Breyer spoke up. "For many years, Congress has passed laws
saying...you cannot discriminate on the basis of race, religion, sexual
orientation. If we were to write an opinion for you, what would we have
done to that principle?"

In reply, Francisco drew on the hypothetical case of a black sculptor
being asked to create a cross for a Ku Klux Klan service. That, he said,
was totally unacceptable. "When you force somebody not only to speak
but to contribute that speech to an expressive event to which they are
deeply opposed, you force them to use their speech to send a message
that they fundamentally disagree with. And that is at the core of what
the First Amendment protects our citizenry against."

That was the end of the solicitor general's time. I felt like we'd landed
in a good place and that he had built well on Kristen's arguments. He
seemed to me to have been effective and compelling in pointing out that
the principle at stake in my case affected all creative Americans who
might be compelled to express ideas through their art that went against
their deepest beliefs.

Then it was time to hear from attorneys for the defendants. This too
would require a dividing of the time allowed; the solicitor general
of Colorado was there to defend the state and its Civil Rights Commission, whose judgment I was challenging based on both a) the discrepancy
between how they treated me and others charged with the same complaint, and b) their explicitly hostile attitude toward my freedom of
religion. The ACLU attorney, David Cole, was on hand to speak more
specifically for David and Charlie.

From the start, it was clear that Yarger's job was not going to be easy.
Those scraps of hostile language the commission employed to describe
religious freedom as something used to justify slavery and the Holocaust

had clearly struck a chord with the justices, who peppered him with questions about these and other statements. Yarger ended up having to spend a significant portion of his time defending the Civil Rights Commission, trying in vain to move some of the justices past the words of the commissioner who had described my references to religious freedom as a "despicable piece of rhetoric."

Kennedy, in particular, pressed hard on the way the commission had talked about my First Amendment rights. "Commissioner [Diann Rice] said that freedom of religion used to justify discrimination is 'a despicable piece of rhetoric,'" he said. "Did the commission ever disavow or disapprove of that statement?"

No, Yarger said—there had been no disavowals of that statement.

"Did you disavow or disapprove of that statement?" pressed Kennedy. I think Yarger began to perspire.

"I would not have counseled my client to make that statement."

"Do you now disavow or disapprove of that statement?" Kennedy's voice was firm.

"I...I...I do, yes, Your Honor." The state solicitor general dropped his gaze, as though he wished he were somewhere else at that moment rather than standing at that lectern, having to say words he knew could be seriously damaging to his own argument.

Kennedy was unrelenting, pushing on with his line of questioning about the commission's conduct.

"Suppose we thought that in significant part at least one member of the commission based the commissioner's decision on...hostility to religion," he said. "Could your judgment then stand?"

Suddenly, I was watching a hole open in the other team's defense. From his question, even I could tell that Kennedy was open to the possibility that the commission's decision against me grew out of an atmosphere that was openly hostile to my religious beliefs—and therefore fundamentally flawed.

Finally, Yarger stepped back from the podium and sat down. It had not been Colorado's best day at court. I was pretty sure that his argument

did not go the way he expected. I was glad his points seemed to fall short
of convincing some of the justices.

The attorney for David and Charlie was the next to step up to the bar.
The justices seemed a little worn down now; the questions came less
frequently than for those who had spoken earlier. In his arguments, Cole
insisted that, under Colorado law, I didn't have the right to choose which
messages I would use my art to express. My lawyers believe he missed
entirely the point that states sometimes can and do apply laws wrongly,
or in ways that lawmakers never intended. My case was proof of that.
Colorado applied a law in a way that compelled my speech, something
that under the U.S. Constitution, no state government has the power or
authority to do. Neither I nor anyone else should be forced to express
messages that go against our deepest beliefs.

After the drama of their confrontation with the Colorado solicitor
general, the justices' questions for Cole seemed relatively mild. In a few
minutes, it was over.

Or almost over. As invited by Roberts, Kristen stepped to the lectern
again to present her closing remarks as a rebuttal. Before Kristen
could speak, though, Sotomayor—who a few years later would officiate
a same-sex wedding—began peppering her with questions again, and
the mood grew tense.

Still, I thought Kristen made a strong (and ultimately persuasive)
argument when she reminded the court that "the Compelled Speech
Doctrine and the Free Exercise Clause [are] anchored in the concept of
dignity and speaker autonomy. And in this case, dignity cuts both ways.
The record is clear on that.

"Demeaning Mr. Phillips's honorable and decent religious beliefs
about marriage, when he has served everyone and has a history of declining
all kinds of cakes unaffiliated with sexual orientation because of the message, he should receive protection here as well," she continued.

"Political, religious, and moral opinions shift. We know that. And this Court's dedication to [the] Compelled Speech Doctrine and to free exercise should not shift."

Kristen ended with these words:

"A wedding cake expresses an inherent message…that the union is a marriage, and is to be celebrated, and that message violates Mr. Phillips's religious convictions. Thank you. This court should reverse."

She had barely spoken those words when Roberts brought his gavel firmly down. "Thank you, counsel. Case is submitted," he said.

Now it was over.

Nothing said in that last, crowded hour seemed especially new. I'd heard most everything, at one point or another, in other courts and contexts. I believe in marriage between a man and a woman. I believe in serving anyone and everyone who comes into my shop. I can't create custom cakes that send a message of celebration for same-sex weddings because I believe in the biblical definition of marriage. The Constitution protects my right to make that decision, because it protects my freedom of speech and freedom of religion. We had been saying those things in interviews and videos, on talk shows and cable news programs, for years.

Still…this was the U.S. Supreme Court. By the longest of long shots, my God and my country had given me the right, as a citizen, to speak my piece here, in our nation's greatest hall of justice. As I watched the justices file back out through the folds of that tall, red curtain, I knew at least five of them would have to agree on a verdict—including one or two whose legal history and specific questions in the courtroom that day gave me no clear clue as to whether, in the end, they'd be standing with or against me.

But the questions were all asked now. The opposition had made its points, and my lawyer had presented our case clearly, ably, succinctly. There was nothing for it now but to wait and pray.

And trust God for the verdict to come.

21

Aftermath

The courtroom emptied quickly. The ADF team, their guests, Barronelle, and my family all gathered and moved out into the great hall toward the tall bronze doors at the front of the building.

Kristen and I were supposed to go out first. At the top of the steps, I looked out at the U.S. Capitol across the street—beautiful even under the overcast sky. Between it and us, at the bottom of what seemed at that moment a great height, stood several hundred people. A swarm of media, jockeying their cameras and microphones. A group of U.S. senators and representatives, with their aides and security officers, turning from those cameras to look up at us. Amid a sea of "We've Got Your Back, Jack" signs, I spotted the faces of friends, family, and countless strangers— some clearly on our side, some clearly not—chanting and yelling and applauding, or just smiling and waving and waiting for us to join them.

We started down the great marble steps, and it felt like descending Mount Everest. Kristen had my arm, and all I could think of was her high heels and what would happen if I somehow pulled her off balance. *Don't trip this woman,* I kept thinking. *Don't mess this up.* Somehow we managed to walk, smile, wave, and reach the bottom without tumbling, Debi and the rest of our group close behind us.

Looking around at the sea of familiar faces, I was overwhelmed by the renewed realization that I hadn't come to this great court alone. All around me were fellow ADF clients who were facing the same judicial challenges I was for acting on their faith.

There was Kelvin Cochran, the fire chief of Atlanta whose privately published devotional book had cost him the job he loved because it referenced the Bible's perspective on homosexual behavior and marriage as the union of one man and one woman.

Carl and Angel Larsen, whose incredibly successful filmmaking business in St. Cloud, Minnesota, was endangered because they wanted to use their artistic skills to promote that same biblical idea of marriage.

Blaine Adamson, whose popular printing shop in Lexington, Kentucky, faced boycotts when he declined to create messages supporting an LGBT pride event in his community.

And Barronelle, whose flower shop had become the eye of its own legal hurricane after she declined to create special floral art celebrating her friend's same-sex wedding.

All of us faced the same media onslaughts, the same legal storms, the same cold shoulders from government officials and so many in our respective communities. Over the last few years, we and a handful of others had become a close-knit community of friends and fellow believers who strengthened each other in our faith in Christ and encouraged each other with surprise visits, timely gifts, gracious notes, and cheering phone calls. We continue to pray for each other faithfully. We lean on each other.

That morning, while I sat and listened to Kristen argue so effectively on my behalf, most of them were out on the court steps, leading a host of supporters to cheer and pray for what was going on inside. Most of them are no more comfortable in the limelight than I am, yet they made their speeches and endured the catcalls and fielded the questions of impatient reporters. Each of them has had more than their share of unwanted intrusion already—they know as well as I do what it is like to receive the hateful phone calls, the unprintable emails. Yet there they were, publicly identifying themselves with me in a way that could only bring more of that kind of abusive attention down on themselves.

Most of them were on a similar legal track, and any one of their cases could have been the first heard at the Supreme Court. In days to come, any one of them still might land there. But they weren't on those court steps for themselves. They were there to encourage Debi and me. On that December morning, it meant more than I will ever be able to tell.

Standing with them were so many beaming members of the ADF team—attorneys, media relations staff, donors, and supporters from all over the country. It was chilly out on that crowded sidewalk, yet they'd braved the elements and the jostling, the yelling, and the unkind remarks to stand for hours, praying for me and waiting to cheer me as we stepped out into the unknown and the long wait ahead.

Nearby, I saw my sisters, Trish and Linda. I felt Debi's hand in mind, Lisa whispering in my ear, and tears filled my eyes. This was the Lord's good doing. He had brought me up here, as the old hymn says, "through many dangers, toils, and snares." A quiet cake artist from Colorado, and there I was at the nexus of a great legal controversy, the focus of national attention, in the center of a growing circle of remarkably generous, loving friends.

God is good, and His mercies indeed never cease.

Stepping up to share a few remarks with the reporters, I kept thinking how much I did not want to mess that up. *Don't let me say anything wrong,* I kept praying. *It's about You, Lord, not me, and all of this should be about You.*

The ADF team had prepared a podium for the rally speakers, and the media gathered now for me and Kristen, Barronelle, and ADF president Mike Farris. Off to my right, David and Charlie and their supporters were holding their own rally. I couldn't help noticing—and taking some pleasure in the fact—that there were at least three times as many people standing with us as I saw gathered around them.

I took a deep breath, my notes tightly gripped in my hand, bracing myself for the coming barrage of questions. The arguments might be over, but for me, the hearing was about to begin.

As big as the moment was, though, I honestly don't remember all that much of the next few minutes. I do remember facing a bank of microphones, and, as encouraged, speaking about what had happened and what the last five years had cost us.

"It's hard to believe," I said, "that the government is forcing me to choose between providing for my family and employees and violating my relationship with God. That is not freedom. That is not tolerance."

I remember trying to describe what it means to me to create a custom wedding cake, and how my art is an inevitable extension of my faith in Jesus Christ. My emotions, already running high with the excitement of the day, finally caught up with me as I spoke of the sanctity of marriage. The lump rising in my throat nearly choked me, and I had to bite off that last word:

"I've spent many years honing my craft as a cake artist, combining baking with my love of sculpting, painting, and sketching. And I love my craft, because I get to turn a cake into a canvas. Designing them, creating them, allows me to use my artistic vision to create works of art that are beautiful and distinctive, and that mark the beginning of something sacred..."

Kristen stepped up next and, as always, summed up the essence of our case very forcefully and especially well:

"As Justice Kennedy said today during our argument, 'Tolerance is essential to a free society'—and Colorado has not been tolerant nor respectful of Jack Phillips," she said. "So the ACLU's position today and the Colorado government's position today was that they can compel filmmakers, graphic designers, oil painters to violate their conscience and speak messages that violate their convictions.

"This court has never—never—compelled artistic expression or ideological speech, and if it does so now, it will lead to a less pluralistic, less diverse, and less tolerant society. We are hopeful that the court will rule in favor of Jack Phillips and the right of all creative professionals to express messages that are consistent with who they are, and to serve all people, which is exactly what Jack and Barronelle do."

A few minutes later, one reporter asked for my takeaway on the morning. I was most of the way through my reply when the emotions caught up with me again.

"I think it went well," I said. "I just hope now that the justices will look at this case and allow creative professionals like me to create freely according to their conscience . . . and that no one else will have to go through what my family and I have gone through for the last five years."

Despite those moments of emotion, the biggest thing I remember, looking out at all those faces and cameras, is a remarkable, inexplicable sense of calm. Nothing on earth could account for the incredible peace I felt standing on those steps after the oral arguments were over. I tried to explain this to the other reporters as they peppered me with questions. As I told one:

"The most important thing I knew I'd learned in this five-year ordeal was about God's sovereignty. He orchestrates everything. If we're patient, He'll work out His will for us. You know, it's like being in the eye of a hurricane, it's really calm, and I felt like I was standing in the middle, watching everything whirl around me, but knowing He was with me there, too."

That was all true. And it would remain true in the months ahead, as we waited to hear the court's decision. We'd taken the last risk; we'd done everything we could do. If the court decided against us, there was nowhere else for us to go except the throne of God.

As the press conference finally broke up, we made our way to another nearby rally, again to draw encouragement from the loud and cheerful support of our family, friends, and ADF team members. Then we headed back to the ADF offices for lunch, some debriefing and reflections, and more than a few sighs of relief. That evening, we were guests at a great banquet of hundreds of ADF friends and supporters, celebrating the culmination of so much long and hard preparation, litigation, and effort.

After that full, wonderful day, nearly all of us, I'd bet, slept better that night than we had the night before.

My family and I took some time over the next day or two to enjoy the sights of Washington, D.C. Then we packed up, said our goodbyes, and headed home to Lakewood to wait. And wait. Praying for the justices as they sorted out their opinions, wondering what the ruling would be...and what, in the end, all of this would mean for me and my family.

A 1956 family photo, taken shortly after I was born. Clockwise from left: My brother Gary, Dad (holding my sister Linda), Mom (holding me), my sister Patsy (whom I've always called Trish), and my brother Glen. *Jack Phillips Collection*

Third grade, 1964. I was a pretty happy kid—even if my teacher did accuse me of "diarrhea of the mouth and constipation of the brain." *Jack Phillips Collection*

At age thirteen in 1969, with one of my all-time favorite Christmas gifts: a drawing table I would continue to use until after my own children left home. *Jack Phillips Collection*

A family portrait from my high school years, circa 1973. Clockwise from left: Me, Dad, Gary, Mom, Glen, Trish, and Linda. *Jack Phillips Collection*

Graduation, 1974. You can see the uncertainty in my eyes. Golden Cream Donut Company—and my future—were only days away. *Jack Phillips Collection*

Debi and me early in our courtship, 1976. *Jack Phillips Collection*

A year later, we were expecting our son. *Jack Phillips Collection*

Another year later, I had my hands full with Jeremy. *Jack Phillips Collection*

A few samples from over the years that illuminate the difference between "baking a cake" and the artistry I offer.
Jack Phillips Collection

With my children in 1984. From left: Jennifer, Lisa, and Jeremy. *Jack Phillips Collection*

Debi and me in 1985, not long after we came to know Christ. *Jack Phillips Collection*

Working at Child's gave me more opportunities to fine-tune my cake creativity. A "salad" cake I made for a local restaurant's anniversary celebration, circa 1990. *Jack Phillips Collection*

Masterpiece Cakeshop opened on September 3, 1993. This is my first cake as an independent business owner, fresh out of the oven. *Jack Phillips Collection*

Dad helping me in the kitchen of the Cakeshop, 1994. *Jack Phillips Collection*

Debi and me in the area of the Cakeshop that once showcased our wedding cakes, circa 2002. *Jack Phillips Collection*

A day in the life of Masterpiece Cakeshop. Opening early…
Copyright 2019 by Bruce Ellefson

…creating cakes…
Copyright 2017 by Bruce Ellefson

...interacting with customers...
Copyright 2019 by Bruce Ellefson

...and working alongside my daughter Lisa. *Copyright 2017 by Bruce Ellefson*

With my original attorney, Nicolle Martin. *Copyright 2017 by Bruce Ellefson*

Kristin Waggoner, who argued my case at the U.S. Supreme Court, leads the Alliance Defending Freedom legal team that has had my back since the beginning—from the crucial decision in *Masterpiece I* through the litigations of *Masterpiece II* and *III*. *Copyright 2017 by Bruce Ellefson*

Jeremy Tedesco
Courtesy of Alliance Defending Freedom

Jim Campbell
(now with the Nebraska Attorney General's Office)
Courtesy of Alliance Defending Freedom

Jon Scruggs
Courtesy of Alliance Defending Freedom

Jake Warner
Courtesy of Alliance Defending Freedom

People all over the nation prayed for me as my case made its way through the courts. Behind me is a tangible reminder of those prayers. *Copyright 2019 by Bruce Ellefson*

At a press conference before oral arguments at the Supreme Court on December 5, 2017. That's Baronelle Stutzman standing next to me, another artist and small business owner whose rights of conscience have been threatened by government officials. *Copyright 2017 by Bruce Ellefson*

Speaking to the media after the conclusion of oral arguments. *Copyright 2017 by Bruce Ellefson*

22

Victory

We spent six months waiting to hear how the Supreme Court would decide our case. We waited through the cold Colorado winter and into the unpredictable mountain springtime, when freezing days of snow alternate with days of bright sunshine and warm air. We waited all the way into the beginning of June.

Meanwhile, life continued in what had become our new normal. My business ebbed and flowed with the seasons—extra custom cakes and cookies at Christmas, and again at graduation—and I continued to travel for ADF, speaking before various groups and being interviewed by media around the country, explaining our case and hoping to help people understand how important it was to *them*.

You might think the long wait was especially stressful—an exercise in impatient endurance, where we gritted our teeth to get through the endless days. But it wasn't like that at all. I genuinely felt an immense peace after our arguments. I was content in knowing we'd done everything we could do. That we'd been as faithful as possible and the outcome really was always totally in God's reliable hands.

So the days went by. Every morning (except Sundays) I opened the shop and set about creating the best cakes, cookies, and brownies I could. Debi worked in the back office, helping out behind the counter when things got busy. Those are the best days, getting to work side-by-side with Debi, doing what we each love most about our job: serving others. Lisa and our three granddaughters filled the shop with fun and laughter, snacking on the occasional sugar cookie as they worked on their home-school assignments.

Friends and regular customers kept dropping in, as usual, to see how we were doing and if we'd heard any word on the case. Gradually, summer came on. Days of snow became less frequent. The colors of the cookies and cakes we decorated changed weekly: some became brighter, some softened with more pastels...we began crafting our sugar flowers in soft pinks, yellows, and blues. Graduation season—May—came and went in a flurry. I always enjoy that season and the unpredictable cake requests that come with it.

I wasn't stressing the coming decision at all. More important things were filling my attention that spring: the pleasures of family, the joys of my work, the peaceful reassurances of my faith in the Lord.

The long wait wasn't too surprising. We'd thought from the beginning that our case would be one of the last the court would decide before its recess at the end of June.

Sometime near the end of May, though, my sister Linda sent an email asking if I was still keeping tabs on SCOTUSblog for news on my case. I hadn't been, as I had so much work to occupy my hours and had settled in my mind that my decision would not be announced until late June. But when she asked about it, it seemed like a good idea. So on the days I remembered, I would pull up the blog and check for any news of a coming decision. All I could know for certain was that the Supreme Court term was officially scheduled to end on June 25.

On June 4—a Monday—I headed into the shop a little earlier than usual. I straightened things up, glanced over the day's cake projects, and then took a moment to sit down at the computer and check email. A few minutes into that, it occurred to me to check the latest news on SCOTUSblog.

Almost immediately, I saw the words on the screen: "Looks like we have Masterpiece."

The decision was out.

I could barely breathe. I leaned into the screen, reading as fast as I could, realizing with surprise how much legalese I'd learned over the past six years—I actually understood a lot of what this Supreme Court reporter was writing about. But I didn't need a law degree or a dictionary to understand the first words of that blog: "[The decision]…is reversed…. The court rules that the commission's actions violated the Free Exercise Clause."

We'd won.

After all those long years of losses, threats, angry words, and hostile language from government officials, we'd finally, finally won. And in the arena where it really mattered: the United States Supreme Court, the highest court in the land.

It wasn't even a narrow 5–4 victory, which honestly had been the best I'd ever dared hope for. The justices had actually ruled 7–2 in our favor, with only Ginsburg and Sotomayor dissenting.

I kept reading and rereading the news, trying to absorb it. As the fact of our victory sank in, the reality hit me. Tears came to my eyes. I still could barely breathe, let alone talk. I tried to call Debi, of course, but I was too overwhelmed emotionally to carry on even a simple conversation. I ended up texting her, Lisa, and my sister with the news. I can't remember exactly what the texts said, but I know the words I used didn't even begin to express everything I was feeling.

Then the phone calls started pouring in. Family, friends, acquaintances, people who'd been following the case from all over the country. They were as giddy as I was, eager to shout congratulations, offer encouragement, share the joy. A few of the unpleasant kinds of calls came in as well—not everyone was so pleased with the court's decision—but the profanities didn't sting. They couldn't make a dent on my wondering, thankful heart.

When things calmed down a little, I was able to begin sifting through all the thoughts and feelings that came flooding in with the decision. And the biggest thing I felt was a deep sense of God's faithfulness.

Make no mistake: God is the hero of this story. The victory is His alone. I felt that so strongly that morning: that God had worked—through me, yes, and through ADF—but God Himself had done all the heavy lifting and brought us to this remarkable moment of joy. My heart overflowed with even greater thankfulness that my family—my wife, our daughter, and most of all, our three granddaughters—had been there in the shop, witnessing God's hand at work all through the years. They'd seen firsthand, in this huge way, the faithfulness of God. I think, after everything, that's what I was most thankful for.

In the days to come, I learned more about why the justices had ruled in my favor.

It turned out that one of the keys to the case had been the Civil Rights Commission's comparing me with Nazis and slaveholders for trying to remain true to my faith. The majority decision—written by Justice Anthony Kennedy—said the commission had failed to show any kind of neutrality about my religion.

Kennedy wrote that "the record here demonstrates that the Commission's consideration of Phillips' case was neither tolerant nor respectful of Phillips' religious beliefs." In fact, as Kennedy pointed out, the Constitution requires representatives of the government—such as the Colorado Civil Rights Commission—to be both of those things when faced with a person's religious convictions.

"Government has no role in deciding or even suggesting whether the religious ground for Phillips' conscience-based objection is legitimate or illegitimate," Kennedy said. In other words, the commission overstepped its bounds when it deliberately and aggressively went after me for my faith in Christ and the truth of the Bible. That disrespect for my beliefs, Kennedy indicated, was a major reason why he and his colleagues ruled in my favor.

A second element was also crucial to the case: the commission's decision to treat me differently than the other cake designers who, like me, had opted not to design custom cakes because they couldn't agree with the message requested.

Kennedy brought up those three other cake designers who declined to create cakes expressing opposition to same-sex marriage. He wrote about how the commission had rejected my choice and my reasons while embracing theirs—even though our rationale was identical. The commission had upheld their rights to choose which messages to express through their creations, while bluntly denying me those same rights. That disparity—and hypocrisy—had prompted Kennedy and most of the other justices to rule in my favor.

Kristen always told me that, no matter what—even after some of those devastating losses in lower courts—I should always look and act like a winner. She'd remind me, bad ruling after bad ruling, that each lower court is just another step toward a higher court. To my surprise, I didn't find that attitude at all hard to embrace. I felt God's presence so strongly throughout the entire case, the whole six years, that even when things were going against us, I never felt like a "loser."

So when we finally won at the highest court and the great struggle seemed finally over, I remember feeling a lot more joy and relief for my family and friends than I felt for myself. I'd watched for years as the case took such a heavy toll on them, and now to see that they could rejoice in this clear demonstration of God's love...that was the best victory of all.

Around 2,500 years ago in Babylon, three men stood before a king named Nebuchadnezzar. They were Jews, the people the Babylonians had conquered and carried back home into slavery. Nebuchadnezzar required all the people in his kingdom to worship a great golden idol he had created—and his captives, of course, were no exception. Yet when the time came to bow and worship this god, three young Jews refused to do so. They would not give a false god the glory and authority reserved only for the true One.

The king was not pleased. He warned them: bow or die. And he wasn't kidding. He'd already prepared a great furnace of fire, and anyone refusing to worship the golden idol was to be thrown into that furnace. Nevertheless, these three—Shadrach, Meshach, and Abednego—steadfastly refused.

Beside himself with fury, the king had the furnace heated seven times hotter than usual. He offered the three men one last chance to obey. It's worth noting that he never asked them to recant or disavow their faith—merely to bow down and worship the statue he had set up. Apparently, he felt they could have done both things: bow to the statue and continue to worship Yahweh. Most of the cultures around them would easily have done so. Adding another "god" was no problem for others—so why was this a problem for these three Jews? Their reply has come down through the ages as an inspiration to all who determine to stand for their religious freedom and convictions:

> Shadrach, Meshach and Abednego replied to him, "King Nebuchadnezzar, we do not need to defend ourselves before you in this matter. If we are thrown into the blazing furnace, the God we serve is able to deliver us from it, and he will deliver us from Your Majesty's hand. But even if he does not, we want you to know, Your Majesty, that we will not serve your gods or worship the image of gold you have set up."[1]

Perhaps it will not surprise you to find I have always drawn special inspiration from that story, even before the events of the last few years transpired in my life. Though I'm not Jewish or a refugee like those young men, and I've never been threatened with death by fire, I still identify with the essence of their stand.

Like them, I suffered a great injustice. Like them, I came face to face with a government authority that compelled me to obey laws that conflicted with my faith in God. Like them, I was ordered to communicate a message that I couldn't agree with. Or else.

Of course, Shadrach, Meshach, and Abednego had no court of appeal. They left their fate in the hands of their Creator and trusted Him to accomplish His purpose in whatever happened. I did my best to follow their example—and like them, I came to marvel at God's mercy and rejoice in His triumph over my circumstances.

Another verse from God's Word speaks to a truth we often forget when our circumstances seem to cast us upon the mercy of those in authority: "The king's heart is in the hand of the Lord, like the rivers of water; He turns it wherever He wishes."[2] Those lines remind me again of that extraordinary word "sovereignty." God knows the hearts of kings and presidents, governors and justices, and He moves in the hearts of all of them—those who believe in Him, and those who do not—to accomplish His ultimate purpose.

While the emotions were still swelling from our win, ADF was galvanizing for action: the attorneys quickly had me booked on a two o'clock flight out of Denver to New York to appear on a slew of news shows that night and the following morning.

They also gave me a direct order: "No interviews without an attorney present."

That command came through just about the time all the TV news crews were pulling into the parking lot of my shop. "Can you talk with us?" they asked.

"Nope, sorry—no attorney present. No comment."

They begged and pleaded, but I had my instructions—and a lot of cakes to bake before I headed for the airport. At least one of them settled for a photo of me with a pastor friend, who came by to offer his congratulations—taken through the window.

The next day, I was in Washington, D.C., and learned anew what a difference being a figure in the news could make in your everyday life. I was barely off the train from New York, walking through Union Station, when I received a call from radio host Michael Medved. He wanted to interview Kristen and me there and then, so I found the quietest loud corner I could and obliged.

Between other interviews, I went for a long walk along Pennsylvania Avenue and happened by the Newseum. Gone now, it was at that time a fine archive that paid tribute to the history and great heroes of American journalism. Out in front of the building, which had the First Amendment carved in the marble of its façade, the owners displayed some eighty front pages of newspapers from many major cities around the country and a few from around the world. I noticed that several had led with the story of our Supreme Court win—and started counting. All but fifteen of them featured our story. I took pictures of them on my cellphone.

Standing nearby was a young man, tears running down his face. I asked if he was okay, if I could do anything to help. As it turned out, he was upset over the decision in our case.

"What will this mean for gay rights?" he asked. "What's going to happen to me?"

I told him this decision wasn't really about gay rights—it was about free speech and religious liberty, things every American should cherish. I explained who I was and assured him that I love everyone, including people who identify as LGBT. I offered him my card, telling him to contact me if he'd ever like to talk. So far, he hasn't called.

Not long afterward, a couple asked, "Aren't you Jack Phillips?" I posed with them for a selfie, explaining to them some of the events of the day. They were clearly supportive.

I decided to eat at a Mexican restaurant. After making my selection from the menu, I headed to the counter to pay, only to be told that someone had covered my bill. I went back to my table with the sobering realization that Washington, D.C., is a news-focused city: there was a good chance most of the people in that restaurant and out on the street knew who I was or were discussing my case—or both. And it was possible that half of them hated me.

I'm glad to know I'm not the only one who's benefited from *Master-piece*—and that the benefits have been considerably greater than free tacos. In the years since the high court's decision came down, I've come to realize how broad the impact of its ruling has been for many other artists, business owners, and ministries around the country.

One of the first to benefit was my friend Barronelle Stutzman. Just a few days after the high court's decision in *Masterpiece*, the justices issued a "grant, vacate, and remand order" to the Washington Supreme Court, which had ruled against her. The order directed the Washington justices to formally reconsider the charges against Barronelle in light of their decision in my case.

Early on, there seemed a general perception that Justice Kennedy's opinion was exceedingly narrow—that his concern was more with the hostility shown me by the Civil Rights Commission than the larger issues of free speech and religious liberty.

But over these last few years, *Masterpiece* has been cited in more than eighty court cases, signifying that the decision has broader implications than many first supposed. There seems to be a growing consensus that the Supreme Court sent a message that the government can't kick Christians out of the marketplace—and that it can't treat Christians and others with strong religious convictions any better or worse, based on their faith beliefs. What's more, the *Masterpiece* decision strongly suggests that when government officials offer one group of people certain freedoms and protections under the law, it cannot deny people of faith those same freedoms and protections.

The Supreme Court itself has cited the *Masterpiece* precedent in sending at least two cases—including Barronelle Stutzman's—back to lower courts for review. Other courts have also cited the case—in Michigan, for instance, where East Lansing officials penalized the Christian owners of Country Mill Farms for expressing their biblical view of marriage online. And in New York, where Syracuse officials tried to shut down New Hope Family Services, a Christian-owned adoption agency, for placing children in homes with a married mother and father, consistent with their biblical view that this is in the children's best interest—compelling them, like me, to choose between compromising their faith or being shut down. In both cases, judges drew on our decision and ruled against the government officials.

So the impact of *Masterpiece* is being felt far, far beyond a Lakewood cake shop. And I pray that it will continue to do so for many, many years to come.

Wouldn't that be a wonderful note on which to end my story? I only wish we could. It would be so satisfying to say I'm back to creating custom wedding cakes and that our whole adventure in the legal world is behind us.

But sometimes God doesn't tie things up quite that neatly.

The Supreme Court's announcement on June 4, 2018, marked the end of *Masterpiece Cakeshop, Ltd. v. Colorado Civil Rights Commission*. But even then, as I was expressing my thanks again to Kristen, Jeremy, Nicolle, and so many others, another storm was brewing that would challenge my right to create freely in accordance with my beliefs all over again.

23

Masterpiece II

A s I mentioned earlier, the day we heard the Supreme Court had granted us cert was a lively, crazy one at Masterpiece Cakeshop. Beyond the usual flow of customers and phone orders coming in, we had waves of jubilant friends honking and waving as they drove past, or dropping by or calling in to congratulate us. Journalists kept clamoring for a statement, and we had calls going back and forth with ADF working out travel plans to get me to the East Coast for interviews as soon as possible.

In the midst of all that commotion, someone called the shop, requesting thirty-eight wedding cakes for thirty-eight ceremonies delivered to thirty-eight states—many of them intended to celebrate his so-called "marriage" to a computer. I declined, and he later filed a lawsuit against me for doing so.

That call certainly made an impression, as did another one that came in that morning, also requesting a custom cake. This caller wanted one that was blue on the outside, pink on the inside, to celebrate a gender transition.

Debi knew I'd need to handle that, so she put the caller on hold while she went to get me. By the time I came back to talk with the person, there was no one on the line. Somehow, we'd gotten disconnected. Then the person called back and talked with Lisa, who politely declined the request on my behalf, knowing the message was not one I could communicate.

The caller turned out to be a local Denver attorney, Autumn Scardina, who identifies as transgender. Scardina works in a small practice specializing in family law and anti-discrimination litigation. In fact, this was not the first time Scardina had contacted me. Very shortly after the incident with David and Charlie back in 2012, Scardina had contributed to that first wave of hateful, angry emails I'd received, sending one which specifically described me as a "hypocrite," and another denouncing me as "a bigot."

In December 2016, our phone records indicate that Scardina had apparently tried to call me again—I may never know why.

The Supreme Court's decision to grant cert sparked a surge of strange requests—many of them, oddly, pressing satanic themes: a "happy birthday, Satan" cake (to feature red and black icing and an upside-down cross), a cake with a pentagram, a three-tiered cake covered with cheese-cake frosting with an obscene image of Satan on top of it. (That one came on the day the Supreme Court's opinion was announced.)

Also in the mix, on October 6, 2017—four months after the gender-transition cake request—was another telephone order from Autumn Scardina, this time requesting a custom cake themed with red and black icing and an image of Satan smoking marijuana. I declined to design all these cakes, obviously, because of their intended messages. But clearly, I had been on Scardina's radar for quite a while.

I know all this because two weeks later (and four months before the satanic cake order), on July 20, 2017, Scardina filed a charge against me with the Colorado Civil Rights Division. I was notified of the complaint, and I passed it along to my ADF attorneys, who filed a response on my behalf. Division officials then proceeded to conduct another investigation and decided they had probable cause to prosecute me again—but apparently only after sitting on that decision for almost a year, until the Supreme Court had ruled on my original case in 2018.

So it turned out I was only able to enjoy about three weeks of renewed "normalcy" before opening my mail to find that I was being hauled before the Colorado Civil Rights Commission again. Yes—again.

The first thing I realized upon reading the notice was that these officials had learned absolutely nothing from the high court's decision. The accusation here, again, was that I had no right to decline to create a cake expressing a message that violated my Christian beliefs. The only difference was that this time, my beliefs involved a gender transition rather than a same-sex wedding.

This wasn't confusion on the division's part. The notification even acknowledged that I had declined the request because I did not want to express through my cake art "the idea that a person's sex is anything other than an immutable God-given biological reality." So the officials clearly understood this was a virtual rerun of the case the highest court in the land had just decided in my favor, stating that my religious beliefs deserved tolerance and respect from the government and that I had exactly the same rights as other cake artists to choose which messages to express through my designs.

Nonetheless, the state had determined, once again, that I had probably broken the law.

This time, Jim Campbell and another lawyer named Jake Warner were taking point on my case, and Jake—like Jeremy, Nicolle, Kristen, and Jim—would prove himself a true friend as well as an excellent attorney. He had immediately recognized these latest actions as another attempt by the state to punish me for exercising my First Amendment rights—the very thing the Supreme Court had just chastised them for doing. He confirmed that from the materials they'd sent, it was clear the officials recognized my decision was based not on the caller, but the intended message . . . but that they were going to move forward against me, anyway.

Although Debi was aware of what was happening, I was sad to have to throw cold water on the joy of my other family and friends, who were still so excited over the victory at the Supreme Court. Now I would have to tell them that, in fact, our legal gauntlet wasn't over, and more hard times lay ahead.

My family and I just wanted to be able to run Masterpiece, create our cakes, and serve our customers again without overhanging clouds of litigation. But it seemed God was calling us to something different than that, and if I'd learned anything, it was that following God's calling would never leave me stranded—and, in fact, would only do me good.

This time, my attorneys and I decided on a slightly different strategy. Rather than let state officials set the tone for this case, we decided to go on offense. In the weeks following the notice from the Civil Rights Division, Jim, Jake, and their fellow ADF attorneys prepared a federal lawsuit against the Civil Rights Commission, pointing to the hostility and bias the government continued to show against me, despite the Supreme Court's recent ruling.

While they worked on the lawsuit, we kept the situation pretty quiet. I had already decided that even with the Supreme Court ruling, I was not going to try to reenter the wedding business quite yet. After several years away from it, reassembling all the elements and staff I needed to bring that aspect of my business up to speed could take a while. And, of course, I couldn't help wondering who else might be out there, looking for a way to paint me into another legal corner.

With this new situation brewing, I knew that had been the right decision. The high court justices had upheld my right to the free exercise of religion without undue government interference, but the State of Colorado was still trying to interpret its public accommodations law to discriminate against me. The Supreme Court justices had spoken; Colorado officials chose to ignore them. I needed a federal court to step in and once again stop state officials from treating me differently—and worse—than other cake artists because of my faith.

Isn't that ironic? To keep me from doing what they imagined I was doing—treating customers differently based on my faith—the state was willing to treat *me* differently than other shop owners...based on my faith.

We would claim in our lawsuit that the state had (again) violated my First Amendment right to freedom of speech, my religious freedom, and now my right to due process.

But we weren't quite ready to file just yet. In the earlier situation, David and Charlie had been able to tell their story first—leaving me in the difficult position of having to respond to their accusations. This time, we wanted to tell my story first.

We weighed carefully the risks of filing a federal lawsuit. Generally speaking, federal courts don't want to hear cases that involve an ongoing state investigation, as my case did. They want to stay in their own lane, as it were, and not get involved in state matters unless someone can show that doing so is especially necessary.

But in our case, ADF thought there was more than enough evidence of bad faith and hostility from the government against me personally to convince a federal court to get involved. On those rare occasions when federal courts do get involved in situations like this, that's usually the reason why. Given the circumstances, Jim, Jake, and the other attorneys didn't feel we had much to lose.

So we charted a course back toward the eye of a hurricane. I felt the winds rising again. And I knew once more that I was not alone.

On August 14, 2018, my attorneys filed *Masterpiece Cakeshop Inc. v. Elenis*, a federal lawsuit in the U.S. District Court for the District of Colorado against the members of the Civil Rights Commission, the director of the Civil Rights Division, the state attorney general, and the governor. We were swinging for the fences.

In the suit, we followed the Supreme Court's example, pointing out that the commission was treating me unequally. While allowing three other bakers to decline to create cakes that expressed messages against their beliefs, they steadfastly refused to allow me that same freedom. In weighing the actions of those other bakers, the state judged their objections to be message-based but was adamant that my decisions had been based not on the message involved, but on the character of those asking for the cake. As my attorneys said in the lawsuit, "Colorado continues its practice of treating Phillips worse than other cake artists because it despises his religious beliefs and how he practices his faith."

Strong language, but we needed to take a strong stand. We were challenging state officials who appeared to be deliberately defying a directive from the U.S. Supreme Court. We needed the district court to recognize what the high court had so clearly seen—that not only my First Amendment rights, but also those of countless other Americans were at stake.

Masterpiece Cakeshop was back in court.

24

Dueling with the
Civil Rights Division

W hen we started on this new journey through the courts, I remember thinking hard about why I was doing this—more specifically, why those First Amendment freedoms that the state was trying to take away from me were so important. In all the nuances of the legal arguments, I felt like it was easy to lose track of the basic principles—freedom of speech and freedom of religion—that our judicial system was supposed to protect.

For the average American, freedom of religion means we can believe and practice whatever religious faith we choose, or not follow any faith at all, without having to worry whether the government will come after us for our choice. We take that as a given, but in many parts of the world, choosing to practice a faith the government doesn't approve of is cause for imprisonment—even death.

Our society draws several benefits from upholding our religious freedom. Places of worship and religious organizations provide extensive social services by operating schools, hospitals, soup kitchens, crisis pregnancy centers, drug rehabilitation centers, homeless shelters, adoption centers, and other community outreach programs.

Unlike government-run social services, these religiously based social service programs usually don't cost taxpayers a dime. But it's only because of religious freedom that religious organizations can provide them; if the government begins picking and choosing which groups can live out their beliefs freely and which cannot, it will inevitably stifle some—if not all—of these charitable activities.

This is already happening, of course; consider efforts to force Christian ministries to affirm adoption placements contrary to what they believe is best for the child, or government bans on Christian groups providing hurricane relief to displaced families if they led voluntary prayer services on the side.

Many confuse freedom of religion with freedom of worship—a confusion increasingly exploited by politicians. "Freedom of worship" suggests you can pray to whomever you want, as long as you do so behind closed doors. "Freedom of religion" means the doors stay open, and you can live out your faith in the public square. That's a crucial difference.

Clearly, freedom of religion is closely tied to freedom of speech, which ensures that each individual gets to choose what he or she can and cannot say or express. (Freedom of speech actually covers freedom of silence too.) And this freedom involves all forms of expression, including filmmaking, songwriting, dance, design (including floral art and T-shirts), and yes, cake artistry.

Even though some protests and demonstrations have pushed the extreme boundaries of freedom of speech (think flag burning), the principle certainly remains sound and worth defending. Each of us has the freedom to lift our voice, wiggle our pen, and click our computer keys about ideas and issues we believe in without being forced to create messages or speak in support of those we don't.

Without this freedom, there could be no "marketplace of ideas" in which we weigh the truth of what's said and written and decide our beliefs for ourselves. Instead, we'd be locked in an endless echo chamber, hearing only what those in charge want us to hear, saying only what they want us to say, believing what they have determined we should believe.

We saw this principle in action as recently as October 2020, when social media platforms locked the accounts of news outlets and individuals sharing an unflattering story about a presidential candidate's son. That's a deadly path for any society to go down. Free speech is especially essential for democracy—which is why it's the first liberty to disappear when a tyrant seizes control of a nation.

All of this shaped and colored both of my cases as I struggled to retain my First Amendment right: listening to my conscience, acting on my faith in Jesus Christ, choosing for myself whether the messages others would compel me to create violated the convictions I hold dear.

We are "endowed by our Creator with certain unalienable rights," our Declaration of Independence says. And the loss of our freedoms begins with just one person surrendering those sacred rights to the whims of an overreaching government. I am not willing to be that person. I count the blessings of liberty we've been given as my birthright as an American, and more than that, as the birthright of my children and grandchildren. I believe those rights are worth fighting for—once, twice, or as often as the ongoing struggle for freedom requires.

After we filed our federal lawsuit, we heard little for nearly two months. Finally, on October 9, 2018, I learned that based on its investigation of Scardina's complaint, the commission had decided to formally prosecute me a second time.

I was ordered to attend a hearing before an administrative law judge on February 4, 2019, who would then decide whether I had violated the Colorado Anti-Discrimination Act by declining to create a cake with a message for Scardina that I would not express for anyone. The list of possible penalties was a virtual repeat of those I'd been threatened with before. My life seemed stuck on replay: same commission, same charges, same procedures...just a different date on the calendar.

Clearly, the commissioners were not backing down. Not chastened by a Supreme Court ruling and not intimidated by a federal lawsuit, they seemed determined to keep railroading me until they drove me out of business, once and for all.

The next day, they made their next move: The state responded to our federal lawsuit with a motion of its own to dismiss.

That made for a lot of moving pieces on the legal chessboard now, and it was getting hard to keep track of them. All the players seemed to be adopting new strategies.

The federal lawsuit put a roadblock in the commission's attempts to punish me, and they wanted it out of the way. If the state could convince the district court to dismiss our case, it would have a clear path to proceed with hanging me out to dry.

State officials said pretty much what we might have expected them to say—basically, that because there was an ongoing state case, the federal government needed to stay out of the way. My attorneys said this was the logical course for the state to take, since in the vast majority of cases, the federal court would probably agree with that argument. Still, my case had its share of unusual elements; there was just a chance that the federal court might opt to step in, anyway.

The state officials' motion to dismiss indicated two things: One, that they wanted the federal court to stay out of their way. And two, that they did not want to conduct their own inquisition alongside or concurrently with the federal case. The state wanted to be in the driver's seat, keeping the focus on me and the charge against me. Officials did not want our lawsuit to keep reminding people of the state's deeply hostile attitude toward my faith.

Did that mean they considered that hostility their Achilles heel? If so, we would lean on that weak point as hard as we could.

It took twenty-nine pages for the Civil Rights Commission to explain to the U.S. District Court of Colorado why our federal lawsuit should be dismissed. The state just didn't seem to understand the Supreme Court's ruling in my earlier case. Instead, it claimed that the high court's decision had nothing to do with this new charge against me—no matter how nearly identical the charges might seem. Apples and oranges, the state insisted, demanding that our whole lawsuit be thrown out, the federal court step aside, the Supreme Court be ignored, and the commission be allowed to continue its quest to eliminate my freedoms.

To drive home the point, the commission bore down hard on the fact that this was a state issue, that state processes were more than adequate for handling the case, and that however much the Supreme Court might be concerned that the Centennial State was looking to punish me out of a peculiar loathing for my Christian faith, nothing could be further from the truth. Their determination to prosecute me while excusing three other bakers for doing the exact same thing for the exact same reason had nothing—nothing—to do with the fact that I alone based my decision on my personal religious convictions.

All of which, to me, seemed like pretty clear evidence that the state had an enormous blind spot when it came to its actions toward me—and that its processes, in fact, were not at all adequate for handling this case.

For their part, my attorneys were mulling over a couple of options. One, we could just respond to the motion to dismiss with our own arguments and then wait and see what the federal court decided. Two, we could raise the stakes. ADF felt like we'd put up with enough—more than enough—by then. It was time, the lawyers said, to confront the state officials' attempts to suppress my freedom and stop them in their tracks.

So they drafted what's called a motion for preliminary injunction. This motion basically asked the federal court to stop state officials from prosecuting me and treating me worse than other cake artists for however long the lawsuit continued—which, as I had learned the first time around, could be a very long time, indeed.

In other words, we were asking the federal court to tell the commission to leave me alone until the federal court could decide whether or not the state had a right to single me out for my faith.

In our motion, ADF attorneys made it absolutely clear that we should win the federal lawsuit. We had strong footing to argue on three separate claims: free exercise (of my religion), free speech, and due process (fair hearing). Basically, we could prove that my religious freedom was being compromised, my free speech was being violated, and my right to a fair hearing was being ignored.

The case for that last one was becoming increasingly easy to document. We had, of course, the heinous comments made by Civil Rights Commission members during the previous case—particularly when past commissioner Diann Rice called my faith "despicable rhetoric" and compared it to the beliefs that led to slavery and the Holocaust. Even after the Supreme Court condemned those comments, Rice, after leaving the commission, doubled down on those comments, writing an opinion piece in which she did not back away from her words. In addition, former commissioner Raju Jairam said I should not be allowed to do business in the state because of my beliefs, and former commissioner Katina Banks went on record to support him in that claim. No commissioner pushed back against any of these awful things being said about me.

While none of these people were still sitting on the commission in 2018, the current members were already expressing the same aggressive dislike for me. Back in 2013, before she joined the commission, Jessica Pocock referred to me as a "hater" in a series of tweets. During my previous lawsuit, Commissioner Anthony Aragon had posted Facebook comments about the case along with a picture of a rainbow White House—making clear his predisposition to support same-sex marriage and oppose anyone who did not. He was also part of a group that filed an amicus brief against my case at the Supreme Court.

All of that helped my attorneys show in our motion for preliminary injunction that even though the commission had changed its members, it certainly had not changed its ways and continued to treat me worse than other cake artists.

Why ask for the preliminary injunction instead of just waiting for the case to play out? Because, my attorneys pointed out, my constitutional rights were being violated every single day that the commission insisted on treating me with hostility. The commission's actions had become so egregious that we needed a federal court to step in and uphold my rights—and we couldn't wait, possibly for years, until the case was resolved for that relief.

We filed our motion for a preliminary injunction on October 25, parallel to the state's motion to dismiss. The state was asking the federal government to stay out of the whole process and let the commission handle it; we were asking the federal government to step in and shut down the commission's prosecution until our federal lawsuit was resolved. (After all, if the federal lawsuit wound up being settled in our favor, the commission likely would be unable to pursue its case, anyway.)

That left a lot for the federal court to sift through and decide, and we waited eagerly for its decision.

25

A Lively Day in Court

I was still marveling that the state had any case at all at this point. There didn't seem to be any way for Colorado officials to misconstrue the Supreme Court's intent or squirm out from under its explicit directive: respect this man's rights, lay off of his religious views, and respect his freedoms as much as those of any other cake artists.

Like most Americans, I'd assumed that once the Supreme Court ruled on something, it was set in stone. I took it for granted that all state and local governments around the country would come to attention, salute, and respect the court's decision. It hadn't occurred to me that some government officials, like those on the commission, might just opt to ignore or look for ways around a ruling they didn't like. That they might actually get away with misinterpreting the ruling, or with arguing that what the justices said didn't apply in certain situations. Or that in those situations, someone needed to step in, underline what the court's ruling meant, and hold everyone accountable for applying it.

That was my situation: we needed someone, in this case the U.S. District Court for the District of Colorado, to clarify how the state could and could not treat me following the ruling by the U.S. Supreme Court.

The district court hearing was set for December 18—just over a year after my appearance in Washington, D.C. Jim Campbell and Jake Warner represented me at the hearing. Jim delivered the argument. Senior U.S. District Judge Wiley Y. Daniel presided over the proceedings. The state's motion to dismiss and our motion for a preliminary injunction were both on his plate. It was going to be a long day.

As it happened, we'd already engaged in a scuffle with the State of Colorado at this same courthouse just a month earlier. As my attorneys were preparing for our day in court, another attorney had filed a request for access to some public records on my behalf. We thought these records might help clarify some of the nuances of the situation and serve to strengthen our case. But even though the information was in the public record and we had a right to look at it, the state tried to block our request, citing the ongoing litigation. So in November, ADF attorney Jon Scruggs found himself arguing before U.S. Magistrate Judge Scott T. Varholak that we should be granted access to these records. The judge agreed.

Consequently, when my attorneys walked through the doors of the Denver federal courthouse on December 18, 2018, it was with some hope and hard-earned confidence.

Which is not to say we didn't have our off moments. Flying in from Scottsdale the afternoon before our court date, Jake and Jim came equipped with everything they'd need to present a compelling argument before the judge: documents, folders, records, etc. What they didn't bring was a tie for Jim. You can get away without wearing a tie these days in most places—even church or the office. But you still have to wear one if you're a lawyer standing before a judge. Jake and Jim added a quick shopping trip to their evening preparations.

The next morning, the two made it to court in time to meet opposing counsel before the arguments started. The state had enlisted some formidable legal talent to argue on its behalf: three assistant attorneys general and one assistant solicitor general. Clearly, Colorado officials were taking this case very seriously.

It quickly became apparent to all of them that Judge Daniel had done his homework. He came prepared with perceptive, probing questions. He asked Jim, for example, why we had chosen to include then Governor John Hickenlooper as one of the defendants in our lawsuit. Jim explained it was because the governor had chosen the commissioners who had shown themselves so hostile to me. He was therefore a key element in our due process argument.

Daniel then walked both parties through the case; Jim and Jake were pleased to note some of the details he elected to mention. He brought up the difficulties we'd faced gaining access to public records early. He referenced our previous victory at the Supreme Court—an indication, perhaps, that he agreed with us that its ruling controlled our current situation.

He then briefly discussed the First Amendment rights in question: free speech, free exercise, and due process, then got down to the meat of the hearing: the state's motion to dismiss.

Daniel began burrowing into the question of whether there was reason enough for the federal government to barge into what was basically a state case. He asked my attorneys to submit their evidence of the commission's bad faith or harassment. Jim immediately began detailing examples of both—but the judge suddenly seemed inclined to move on from that question, although Jim said he had more information to present.

The judge said he could go ahead, but, "Don't talk so fast…the court reporter goes crazy." That drew a smile from the audience and told my attorneys that Daniel wanted to move this case along. He'd read the briefs carefully and already knew most of what he needed to know. He did ask questions, though, and some of them suggested he might be considering denying the state's motion.

Jim cited more biased commissioners, more hostile comments against me on social media, the problems with the commission's hearing process (where the same commissioners could accuse me on the front end of a trial and judge me on the back end). He also suggested that the nature of Scardina's cake request had the appearance of a setup. And, given the division's decision to wait nearly a year before acting on his accusations and completely disregarding the Supreme Court's ruling, it seemed increasingly likely that state officials had decided to be complicit in that setup.

At that point, Daniel stopped Jim's presentation, indicating he'd heard enough from our side about whether the commission had acted in bad faith. He was ready to hear from those representing the commissioners. Colorado Assistant Attorney General LeeAnn Morrill rose to tell the judge that we had things all wrong—that my team's argument was based on mistaken assumptions about the state officials' beliefs or motivations. She assured him that, in fact, nothing in the commissioners' actions indicated any bad faith at all.

This time, Daniel put the brakes on her. He wanted to zero in, he said, on the question of whether the state was persisting in its policy of treating me worse than other cake artists.

Morrill challenged my attorneys' suggestion that the commissioners were ignoring and/or disrespecting the points the Supreme Court had made in its ruling on my earlier case. "I want to be very clear to the court that we don't in any way discount the Supreme Court's holding in *Masterpiece I*," she said. "We have not attempted to treat Phillips unequally." It was her contention that I was basically willing to make a similar-looking cake for some people, but not for others—an idea that disregards a key principle of communication: context matters.

Even when two custom cakes look similar, their messages can vary widely, based on the context. Say a black cake artist is asked to sculpt and create a white, cross-shaped cake to celebrate the anniversary of a Lutheran church down the road. Should the state then have the power to come in and force that same black cake artist to create an identical white cross cake, in order to express a racist message for the Aryan Nations Church across town? Absolutely not. The cakes may look the same, but the messages they send out are worlds apart.

Morrill talked about my custom cakes as if they were mass-produced lumps of batter and frosting just sitting around on a shelf. That's not true at all. They are my art form; I design each one with the goal of communicating a particular message for the customer through the cake—a message of celebration, of sympathy, of encouragement, etc.

Bottom line: Because my custom cakes are art, and because of the expressive process I go through to create each of them, it matters a lot to me what message a cake is going to send. If that message goes against my religious convictions or even my artistic beliefs, I can't express it. That's my simple test—a test so simple and yet one the state just could not seem to grasp.

In the minutes that followed, Daniel homed in on a different aspect of Morrill's comments: those about the commission not discounting the Supreme Court's ruling in *Masterpiece I*. It became clear that he saw that the commissioners' current behavior distinctly echoed what Justice Anthony Kennedy had condemned in writing the Supreme Court's majority opinion.

He also quoted Justice Neil Gorsuch's concurring opinion, which noted the commission's willingness to attribute the other three bakers' decisions to their disagreement with the customer's messages—even while insisting that my choice was spurred by "the sexual orientation of the parties involved." Gorsuch called that an "irrational" double standard.

This tack on the judge's part was pretty encouraging for our side. We grew even more encouraged when he said, "I'm going to make a ruling. Let's assume that I deny the motion to dismiss. This case needs to get on a forward track, and so that's why sooner rather than later I'm going to make a ruling." That certainly sounded better for us than for the state.

That statement pretty much ended discussion on the motion to dismiss. Next came our arguments on our motion for a preliminary injunction asking the judge to block the state from proceeding with its case until the federal government made a decision on the commission's ability to act fairly.

The judge listened attentively to our arguments but said he couldn't grant us the preliminary injunction because he believed our request was too broad.

Giving us an injunction, he said, would essentially be the same as ruling on the merits of our federal lawsuit, which was not what this hearing was about. What we could do, he suggested, was file a new motion for a preliminary injunction—one tied to some more specific aspects of the case.

Jim nodded and sat down, but the opposing counsel was not pleased with the judge's idea. Assistant State Solicitor General Grant Sullivan rose and asked the judge to decide, right then and there, whether we should get any kind of injunctive relief at all. Daniel said that topic was not up for discussion. Sullivan continued to persist.

"I'm not going to do [what you're asking]," the judge said. "You are not listening to me."

Sullivan told the judge he thought our request for an injunction was causing prejudice against the commission and the other state officials named in our lawsuit.

"What I'm telling you," Daniel said, "is you are wasting my time. Do you want me to grant the injunction they have requested?"

"No, Your Honor."

"All right, then listen to what I'm saying. Okay? I want to move this along."

Sullivan then criticized what he called "our delay" (in requesting an injunction) and said Daniel was now encouraging us to file another motion for another injunction—which meant even more delay. "I don't want to suggest that their delay is not a problem," he said. "We think it is a problem."

"You know what I'm inclined to do," Daniel replied. "So if you want to say something that you think you need to say to protect your interests and rights, say it…but say it briefly."

"Well, I want to be helpful to the court, Your Honor," Sullivan said. "So if Your Honor wants to hear argument on the existing [motion for preliminary injunction], I'm happy to do that…"

"I don't," the judge said. "I've already told you three times that I think the request is too broad."

"Then I will sit down, Your Honor, if Your Honor doesn't want to hear any legal argument on the existing [motion for preliminary injunction]." Sullivan sat down.

So the state's attorneys never got to make their arguments against our original motion for a preliminary injunction. Meanwhile, my attorneys were back to square one, looking to develop a new motion for a new preliminary injunction. And despite his evident misgivings, we still had no definitive word from the judge on whether he would grant the motion to dismiss.

As the hearing neared its close, Daniel acknowledged this, saying bluntly, "[A]s I've indicated, I'm inclined to deny the motion to dismiss." We'd be on hold for a while, awaiting his decision—but his words and tone gave us hope.

And with that, he announced his court would recess.

26

Another Win

As it turned out, we didn't have to wait for months to learn what Judge Daniel was thinking. On January 4, 2019, he issued his decision on both the state's motion to dismiss and our motion for a preliminary injunction. Our hopes from the hearing had been justified.

Daniel ruled that based on the evidence that the commission was still treating me unequally, our case could go forward in federal court. ADF quoted his reasoning in a press release that read, in part:

> While the state "allow[s] other cake artists to decline requests to create custom cakes that express messages they deem objectionable and would not express for anyone," Colorado treats Phillips differently. This "disparate treatment," the court said, "reveals" the state officials' ongoing "hostility towards Phillips, which is sufficient to establish they are pursuing the discrimination charges against Phillips in bad faith, motivated by Phillips'...religion...."

The state's motion to block our federal lawsuit was denied.

Believe it or not, this decision, in its way, meant almost as much to my attorneys and me as the earlier Supreme Court decision. With that, we felt we had climbed our way, inch by inch, to the top of a huge, legal mountain. Then, when the commission filed eerily similar charges against me, it seemed as if we'd rolled all the way back down to the bottom and might have to start the weary climb all over again. Nothing seemed any different: the commission was still coming after me, still holding me to a different standard, still targeting my freedoms of speech and conscience. If Daniel had chosen to side with them and dismiss our lawsuit, our hands would have been tied and our options sorely limited; we really would have had no choice but to begin the long slog back up to the higher courts again.

Now we still had work to do, but the entire landscape had shifted. We weren't back at the bottom of the hill—we could pick up where we left off, with the Supreme Court's decision (and now Daniel's) giving us new strength and momentum for whatever came next.

What Daniel's decision affirmed was that the Supreme Court's ruling did have an impact on the current lawsuit, and another legal authority saw it as plainly as we did: the commission was being just as abusive now as it had been the first time around. Even better, the new ruling gave us permission to challenge the commission—to move from defense to offense and keep moving forward.

For me personally, it also felt like affirmation that God was still moving my circumstances. I wasn't just caught in a time loop, reliving the lessons of the last six and a half years. He seemed to be subtly giving my attorneys and me the platform to speak out against the commission's unfair attitudes and practices—and to set some new precedents that might eventually impact similar religious freedom lawsuits already working their way through the courts. If we could keep this commission from ignoring my right to live and work in accordance with my beliefs, maybe we could provide other believers with the legal precedent they needed to stop other government officials from inflicting similar abuses on them.

So our next step would be to ask a federal court to consider the commission's latest charges in the light of the Supreme Court's decision—to block these officials from hounding me for my beliefs and to let me go back to doing what I loved: designing creative cakes and welcoming everyone who walked through the door of Masterpiece Cakeshop.

On March 4, ADF attorneys and I headed downtown to the Colorado Attorney General's office. There, I was going to be deposed.

A deposition is a pre-trial questioning. It's part of the discovery process, when lawyers are trying to get as much information as they can about a case. The opposing counsel gets a chance to grill me, trying to pry out any loose ends or comments that might help them when we faced off in court.

In all the trials and hearings that I'd been through before, I'd never been deposed. My attorneys warned me that whatever answers I provided to the state's lawyers would be sworn testimony that could be used later during the trial.

While I wasn't particularly nervous about the deposition, I wasn't looking forward to it either. The questions could be difficult, and the atmosphere oppressive. The attorneys could (and likely would) try to confuse or trap me. And all the while, I would know that everything I said could come back to bite me. One misstep—one wrong choice of words—could make everything still to come that much harder.

It was a cold day, and the ground was covered with snow. I was sitting quietly behind our Uber driver on the way to the attorney general's office, watching the world go by, when I suddenly recognized an old praise and worship song coming over the radio that I hadn't heard in decades. I really liked that song. And hearing it just then, I had an interesting experience of slipping outside the present moment—a moment of wary expectations and nagging tension—and remembering all the many, many ways that God had provided for me in the past. I couldn't help but feel as I listened to that song that God was reaching out to gently remind me of His mercies and provisions during other dark hours. He was kindly reassuring me that He was just as present and just as attentive to what I needed right then, in that particular moment, and in the deposition about to begin.

With that deeply renewed sense of peace, I followed my attorneys into the building. We placed our coats and briefcases in a small conference room, and one of the state's attorneys waved us into a larger one where the deposition would take place. I sat at one end of the long conference table while my attorneys sat along my right side. The state's attorneys would sit across from them on the other side, on my left. A court videographer and a court reporter were already sitting at the far end of the table, and they greeted us as we took our seats.

My three attorneys seemed calm and collected, and in my heart, I was still humming the praise and worship song from the car. I could clearly feel God speaking to me, calming my nerves, and giving me strength.

After a moment, three attorneys for the state came into the room. They sat—and then things took an interesting turn. One of the state's attorneys turned to the videographer and court reporter and excused them from the proceedings. I glanced at my lawyers—none of them seemed to know what was up any more than I did.

After the others left, the attorney who had dismissed them turned and said he'd come to talk to us about going in a different direction.

He wanted to discuss a settlement.

The discussion that ensued is confidential, but what it all came down to was—incredibly—ending our case much earlier than we'd expected and much differently than we'd ever dared hope.

We don't know for sure, but my attorneys suspect the sudden settlement was spurred in part from new evidence that our team had uncovered a few days before. Here's what happened.

During the discovery process, ADF attorneys had noticed that the state produced an agenda and minutes from an interesting Colorado Civil Rights Commission meeting held on June 22, 2018—three weeks after the Supreme Court ruled in my favor. According to those minutes, the commissioners had devoted some of the meeting to sharing their personal impressions of the court's decision. Curiously, the actual recording of the meeting was missing from the material provided to my attorneys.

That might have meant simply that there was no recording or transcription of the meeting. For if there had been such a record, we should have already received it as part of discovery. Still, just to make sure, the ADF team went back to the state's attorneys and asked them to give us any records they might still have of that particular gathering. And, in fact, it turned out that there was an audio recording of it after all. The state's attorneys emailed that recording to us just a few days before my deposition.

Listening to it, my attorneys realized that it contained the most important evidence of the entire case. During the meeting, current commissioners—not the ones who had denigrated me and my faith a few years earlier—could be heard expressing their own full endorsement of the hostile comments made about me during *Masterpiece I*—the same comments the Supreme Court had just quoted and condemned in its ruling.

The commissioners hadn't even tried to hide their hearty approval of former commissioner Diann Rice's comments comparing me to Nazis and slaveholders because of my Christian faith. As ADF later wrote in a press release:

> At the June 22, 2018, public meeting, members of the commission discussed the U.S. Supreme Court's ruling. During that discussion, Commissioner Rita Lewis said, "I support Commissioner Diann Rice and her comments. I don't think she said anything wrong." Later, Commissioner Carol Fabrizio added, "I also very much stand behind Commissioner Rice's statements...I was actually proud of what she said, and I agree with her...I'm almost glad that something the commissioner said ended up public and used, because I think it was the right thing."

From this recording alone, it was abundantly clear that, far from changing their policy of hostility towards me, the commissioners had in fact doubled down on it since the Supreme Court ruling. Here we had definite evidence that they still harbored a deep antipathy for both me and my faith, which we could reasonably argue had influenced their decision to bring the new additional charges against me.

Though they couldn't be absolutely certain, my attorneys were convinced that once these comments came to light, the state knew it was more than likely going to lose *Masterpiece Cakeshop Inc. v. Elenis*. The new evidence underscored all our claims of their deep bias against me and would have given my attorneys ample, solid ground on which to argue that my right to freely exercise my religion was not being respected. With this evidence on the table, the state's attorneys likely decided that the best thing to do was to settle.

As part of the terms of the settlement, my attorneys and I agreed to drop the federal lawsuit, while the state, in turn, completely dismissed and abandoned its prosecution in the administrative case against me. After seven years of litigation, I was two for two.

Think about that...two for two against the State of Colorado.

In truth though, we never would have gotten that agreement without Judge Daniel denying the state's motion to dismiss. His decision allowed the case to go on long enough for that missing piece of evidence to turn up in discovery.

For many reasons, I was glad the case wrapped up so quickly; one was that Judge Daniel himself had a chance to see how it all came out in the wash. He passed away unexpectedly only a couple of months later.

After the deposition meeting, my attorney, Jim Campbell, said in a press release: "We hope that the state is done going along with obvious efforts to harass Jack."

Indeed, I did hope that was true. I was more than ready for life to go back to normal. I wanted to be back at the shop, serving customers—

meeting new ones, welcoming old ones back, being known more for my cakes again than for my high-profile litigation.

Even more than that, I wanted to be able to devote my time and attention to my dear family, my friends, and my church, instead of having so much of it sucked into legal actions and court cases, travel and interviews. With this settlement, I'd finally be able to return once and for all to the life I'd known and loved.

Or so I thought.

Once again, I was wrong. Though the state had dropped its charges against me, I had underestimated the depths of one person's determination to punish me.

Three months later, on June 5, 2019, Autumn Scardina filed a new case against me—this time, in Colorado state district court, asking for a monetary judgment against me of more than one hundred thousand dollars in penalties and damages.

Masterpiece III had begun.

27

Masterpiece III

The new complaint picked up where *Masterpiece II* left off, alleging that I violated not one, but two laws—the Colorado Anti-Discrimination Act and the state's Consumer Protection Act—by declining to create a custom pink-and-blue cake to celebrate a gender transition. More specifically, the complaint alleged that by saying I'm happy to serve everybody, I am essentially promising to create every cake.

That could hardly be true. No matter how cheerfully I offer to serve them, people could ask for all kinds of cake creations I'd be unable to create: a cake as big as a house; a cake for twenty-five cents; a cake laced with poison; or, more commonly, a cake that expresses messages against my core beliefs and convictions. This is common sense.

This new complaint again failed to recognize that I declined because of the cake's message—not because of anything about the person requesting it. As my attorney Jim Campbell put it, "This latest attack by Scardina looks like yet another desperate attempt to harass...Jack Phillips. And it stumbles over the one detail that matters most: Jack serves everyone; he just cannot express all messages through his custom cakes."

The media reacted quickly to this third attempt to pursue me in the courts. Laura Ingraham interviewed me and Jeremy Tedesco on her Fox News show, *The Ingraham Angle*, just a few days after Scardina filed the complaint. Jeremy explained the stakes of this third lawsuit, saying, "[People] want to silence [Jack], banish him, ruin him financially, and send a message of intimidation that he has no place in public life."

A defense had to be made. My attorneys buckled down to draft a motion explaining why the new case should not be allowed to continue. They identified several reasons why the court should dismiss the complaint, but they focused mainly on the point that if Scardina disagreed with the outcome of *Masterpiece II*, the more appropriate next step would have been to take it to the Colorado State Court of Appeals, rather than starting all over in a state district court. But Scardina chose to do this instead.

As for the claim concerning the Consumer Protection Act, my attorneys were able to make a strong argument that in this aspect, it rests on faulty logic: Stating I will gladly create cakes for everyone is in fact a promise to create every cake that someone requests. That's just a deeply unreasonable assumption, for the reasons I mention above.

No business owner could stay in business if customers could presume that statements like "everyone welcome" were misconstrued in this way. Saying "I serve everyone" can't possibly mean "I'll create anything a customer requests, no matter what." I really do welcome people of every background, but every custom cake request at some point has to be measured in terms of context, message, cost, availability, etc. That goes for any creative professional who offers custom expression to the public.

As my attorneys pointed out, the complaint asserting I'd violated the Consumer Protection Act "fails because Scardina fails to allege a deceptive practice with any sufficiency or specificity, fails to allege that Phillips was speaking in the course of his business, fails to allege any harm, fails to allege any public impact, and fails to allege causation." And all those things should have been legally evident in order for the case to move forward.

They put all of that into our motion to dismiss, which we filed on July 22, 2019. The court agreed to hear oral arguments in the case, and my attorney Jake Warner presented those arguments on April 9, 2020.

We didn't have to wait long for the judge's ruling. On April 29, Denver District Court Judge A. Bruce Jones denied our motion in part, allowing the case to proceed.

As this book goes to print, we are preparing to go to trial.

A curious thing has happened, though, in the wake of Judge Jones's decision. Another cake designer—this one in Michigan—found herself in the same kind of trouble I was, for exactly the same reasons. But for exactly the opposite point of view.

This cake designer, known in her community for being an LGBT artist, was approached in her Detroit shop with a request to create a cake with a religious message criticizing same-sex marriage. When she declined to accommodate that request, saying it violated her personal views on the issue, the would-be customer indicated he would file a complaint alleging that she had illegally discriminated against him based on his religion. "No more anti-Catholic discrimination," he tweeted. "See you in court."

The event drew widespread media attention primarily because it so closely paralleled the ongoing facts in my case, with one notable exception: the ACLU—whose lawyers had represented David and Charlie in my first case and refused to accept that my own reasons for declining their cake were about the message, not the men—had no problem at all taking the opposite tack in the Detroit baker's case.

"When you are asked to do a particular message, you might be crossing the line of what could be compelled speech," an ACLU attorney explained, "especially if it's offensive." He's exactly right. But he cannot see why that truth applies to me as well as to the baker in Detroit.

"Public accommodation laws were created to protect ethnic and ideological minorities," Jake wrote in response to the Detroit baker's legal echo of my case. "These laws are supposed to be shields, not swords. And from a legal context, no state law can be used to undermine the fundamental rights of people like Phillips and [the Detroit baker] that are protected by the U.S. Constitution.

"It's time to put down the swords," he added, "respect each other despite our differences and let creative professionals pursue their passions in peace. We don't have to choose between Jack Phillips and [the baker in Detroit]. The world is wide enough for both of them."

I would like to think that's true. We'll soon know if the legal system of Colorado can find its way to see it too.

28

Lessons Learned

So what have I learned from all of this?

Perhaps you won't be surprised to hear that the attacks so many have intended to challenge my faith in Christ have, in fact, strengthened it.

The book of Genesis tells the famous story of Joseph, the almost-youngest of twelve brothers who sold him, as a teenager, into slavery. Joseph eventually found himself in Egypt and in prison for something he didn't do. He suffered there for many years before a miraculous turn of circumstances led to his becoming second-in-command to Pharaoh. Not long afterward, a global famine brought Joseph's brothers to Egypt, seeking food...and led them straight to the man they'd betrayed so many years before. When they realized who Joseph was, they trembled to think what he might do them. But Joseph waved their fears aside.

"Do not be afraid," he said, "for am I in the place of God? But as for you, you meant evil against me; but God meant it for good, in order to bring it about as it is this day, to save many people alive."[1]

That's how I feel about the members of the Colorado Civil Rights Commission, who have worked so diligently to ruin my business and disrupt my life. It's not my place to judge them for what they've done or why they've done it. All I know is that in their desire to do me harm, out of their hostility toward my faith in God, they have actually provided me with some extraordinary platforms from which to give testimony to that faith.

In their eagerness to punish my speech, my opponents have actually given me a microphone—even a megaphone—and for all the pain and loss my family has experienced, we are eternally grateful for the opportunities this has given us to grow closer to our Lord and to speak His truth before so many whom we might otherwise never have met.

Another Bible writer says, "Surely the wrath of man shall praise You,"[2] which is an Old Testament way of saying it does men no good to raise their fists at God or the things He allows, because God can turn even our anger into praises for Himself. I believe that has happened in the course of my legal journey.

In truth, I've never really felt like the government officials coming after me through all of this were really angry, deep down, at me. After all, I've never expressed any intention other than to follow as faithfully as I can what the Word of God says. My thoughts on same-sex marriage aren't mine; they're His. If the commissioners of the Civil Rights Division have qualms with anyone, it's Him. I'm just an ambassador, if you like, trying to represent the biblical point of view.

The New Testament tells us that those who try to articulate what the Lord has given them to say have always been "an example of suffering and patience." In fact, "we count them blessed who endure," Scripture says, because in time they will see "that the Lord is very compassionate and merciful."[3]

That is probably the most important thing I've learned: how good God is. I knew He was good before all of this happened, but coming through oppressive days, enduring the death threats, the hate mail, the obscene phone calls and public demonstrations, seeing the tears of my wife and the worries of my children, hearing people call me a bigot and a Nazi, listening while elected officials openly mocked the deepest convictions of my soul—let me assure you, this is when God's mercies abound. This is when He comforts us in the deep places of the soul that only He can reach.

Often enough, He has chosen to comfort me through the love and devotion and patient encouragement of my family, my friends—those who've walked with me through the years and those I've come to know just recently because they are experiencing the same kind of hardships I am for the same reasons. "For none of us lives to himself, and no one dies to himself," the Bible assures us.[4] I have marveled time and again at the kindness expressed by strangers stopping in at my shop, at the encouraging words of an email from the other side of the country, at the thoughts shared in a letter, or a gentle word spoken in passing.

Being in the spotlight has taught me humility, as strange as that may sound, because it's shown me time and again how unworthy I am of the generous support and tender mercies of these souls my Lord has placed around me to offer me tangible expressions of His unfailing love.

This experience has also taught me to be a better listener.

I am, by nature, more task-oriented than people-oriented. Leaning over a cake and creating a beautiful color portrait or pastel landscape or a funny caricature have always been a lot easier for me than making small talk up by the cash register. But what I've experienced over the last decade has taught me a better understanding of something the Apostle Peter urges us to remember:

> But even if you should suffer for what is right, you are blessed. Do not fear what they fear; Do not be frightened. But in your hearts, set apart Christ as Lord. Always be prepared to give an answer to everyone who asks you to give the reason for the hope that you have.[5]

In the days before David and Charlie walked in, I can't honestly say that I was "always ready" to speak up about my faith. Sometimes, but not always. In fact, it was probably easier for me to "not be afraid of their threats" than to "give a defense" to everyone who asked.

But on the heels of all this upheaval, it quickly became obvious, even to me, that God didn't provide me with such a remarkable platform, or such an unusual testimony, so I could hide in the back by the ovens. He wanted me to engage with those who inevitably made their way into our cake shop, either as customers feeling talkative or as curiosity seekers who were wondering just who this fellow is who won't "just bake the cake."

Sometimes, that takes a lot of patience—more than what comes to me naturally. That person across the counter is making the big point they came in to say, and in the back of my mind, I'm thinking, *That last batch of cakes needs to come out of the oven.* But patience also has been a lesson of this experience—whether I was wondering if the Supreme Court would ever take my case, or waiting to hear what they'd finally decided, or wishing the cab driver would make better time getting me to the airport, or wondering if an interviewer was even listening to what I was trying to say…God has been teaching me a lot about staying calm, minding my tongue, resting in Him. The New Testament shares the writer James's thoughts on this too:

> My brethren, count it all joy when you fall into various trials, knowing that the testing of your faith produces patience. But let patience have its perfect work, that you may be perfect and complete, lacking nothing.[6]

The joy, I've found, comes with the opportunities to make new friends—and yes, to share a little of the Lord's love and grace with those He brings day by day into my orbit.

Whether patience has truly had its "perfect work" yet or not, I couldn't say…I suspect there's more than a little perfecting still to come.

But that idea of perfecting does remind me of one other big thing that's been impressed upon me in the course of my long, long trial by fire.

Like most Americans, my understanding of how our country is supposed to work comes from dimly remembered lessons in high school civics classes…three branches of government, checks and balances, the Declaration of Independence, the Constitution, and the Bill of Rights. Some of the finer points had gotten pretty hazy over the years, and some of those ideals that our teachers tried to impress upon us had faded against the sharper impressions of political infighting, social unrest, and cynical journalists profiling cynical elected officials to present skin-deep reports for an issue-weary public.

Now after all these years on the receiving end of civic policy, the law, the courts, and government officials, I've come to some new understandings. Not only of how on the one hand even those we elect to defend our rights can sometimes grievously abuse them, but of how on the other hand the system really can work in exactly the way our Founders intended.

This is a country where a cake designer in a suburban cake shop— condemned and humiliated by state officials, ignored by higher state courts—can send up a legal flare to the U.S. Supreme Court and be recognized, heard, and exonerated.

This is a country where, almost 250 years ago, God gave us wise men who knew enough to anticipate the recurring challenges and enduring threats that continually endanger personal freedom and helped them forge a document the likes of which the world had never seen before to establish our most basic rights and secure our most essential liberties.

That document is one of God's gifts to America, even as this country has been in many ways God's gift to the world. A nation that affirms that all people's rights "are endowed by their Creator," not their government. A nation whose people have been committed from the beginning to forming a "more perfect Union." This nation, like me, retains many imperfections, but so many are working so faithfully to make it better.

Running afoul of the American justice system has shown me a great deal that is wrong—but it has also reaffirmed my faith in the solid foundation of that system. Judges like Anthony Kennedy and Wiley Daniel have reminded me that many of those who sit in our courtrooms are genuinely trying to weigh justice in the balance and to honor the truths that millions of Americans have found "self-evident" across two and a half centuries.

I have risked everything on the mercies of God and the protections afforded by our Constitution—and have found them both worthy of the trust.

Near the end of his gospel, the Apostle John explains that time and space wouldn't allow him to tell us everything he knew about the life of Jesus:

> Jesus did many other miraculous signs in the presence of His disciples, which are not recorded in this book. But *these* are written that you may believe that Jesus is the Christ, the Son of God, and that by believing you may have life in His name.[7] (emphasis mine)

That's also why I've written my book—in the hope that it may give you a new appreciation of who Jesus is, of what His love and grace and goodness have meant in my life, and of what they can mean in yours.

He is indeed the Son of God. A God who loves you enough to send His only Son to die for your sins, to offer you forgiveness and life forever with Him. He can give you purpose—the courage to be the person He created you to be and the strength to accomplish what He calls you to do. He has a great plan for your life, and He freely offers you the joy and peace your heart so ardently longs for.

I know. I put my trust in Him. And even as one who has paid a stiff price for doing that, I can tell you: It has been worth it. Because the thing I've learned most from all of this is who my Savior really is.

I pray you'll learn that too.

Our Client and Our Friend, Jack Phillips

By Kristen Waggoner and Jeremy Tedesco,
Alliance Defending Freedom

It would be hard to overstate the legal implications of Jack Phillips's case and the already far-reaching impact of the U.S. Supreme Court's decision in his favor. As the attorneys who argued his case at the High Court and also at the Colorado Court of Appeals, we would like to detail a few of the most significant points of that victory. But first, a word on why it was important for Jack to write this book.

From the beginning, Jack's case has been bigger than the courts. Almost from the moment David and Charlie stormed out the door of his shop after he declined to create the cake they requested, Jack and his beliefs have been under intense fire from the self-appointed forces of "tolerance"—which is a misnomer, since their goal is to banish from society people who disagree with them. Those who opposed Jack included a small but very vocal and culturally powerful group of radical activists, many members of the mainstream media, the ACLU and its allies, and his own state government, all of which distorted his words and beliefs. He has been accused of being a hater and a bigot. He also has been called other names that we refuse to write and threatened with death in ways that are too gruesome to describe. Sadly, the State of

Colorado engaged in some of these tactics as well, repeatedly likening Jack to racists in the Jim Crow South and describing his religious beliefs as a "despicable piece of rhetoric" when he invoked his constitutional rights to religious freedom and free speech.

These kinds of assertions and tactics were never limited to the courtroom or to Jack as an individual. This language, these names, and these threats were intended not just to instill fear in him, but in every person who dares to stand with him or to give voice to traditional beliefs about human sexuality and marriage.

Opponents denigrated Jack's religious views and viciously attacked his personal character. But as we have seen, God used those false assertions to bolster Jack's case and move the Supreme Court to condemn the blatant discrimination he faced from Colorado officials. Even so, it is wrong for such a caring, decent man to have his character impugned, his reputation smeared, and his story twisted by opponents who hold powerful microphones in the media and the broader culture.

Jack doesn't often benefit from those kinds of platforms. This book, then, is his opportunity to speak his piece and present his true character and convictions to a broader audience. He repeatedly has said he wanted to write this book so people would know the joy his faith has brought him. And he wanted to answer, once and for all, the question so many people have asked: "Why didn't you just bake the cake?"

It was also important for Jack to share his story because the stakes are still so high. Even though the Supreme Court decided in his favor, Jack is still facing legal challenges, thanks to a small group of activists determined to ruin him. They intend to drive Jack—and anyone else who shares his biblical views on human sexuality and marriage—out of the public square and ruin them personally and professionally. And make no mistake, these activists are spurred on by the atmosphere of religious hostility and intolerance the State of Colorado created by prosecuting Jack—twice!—for simply living out his faith.

Americans must understand that this movement is not about tolerance and inclusivity; it is the opposite. It is about ideological uniformity and the purging of any individuals who do not support and embrace radical ideas that undermine our foundational freedoms. Jack loves and serves all people, and he always has. He was attacked simply because of what he believes.

Too often, situations like Jack's are confined to sidebars in news stories or hostile media profiles, which distort the reality that the men and women being attacked for their beliefs are normal, everyday people. People, in other words, like most of those reading this book.

This case was about a state government coercing and silencing those who hold views that certain powerful people and institutions dislike. It is wrong and harmful for government, or private individuals, to use the law as a tool to tell people what they can and cannot say—to compel them to celebrate ideas and ceremonies that violate their core beliefs. This is as true for Jack as it is for the cake artist who identifies as gay and does not want to celebrate marriage as exclusively between one man and one woman, the pro-life photographer who declines to promote a Planned Parenthood rally, or an atheist writer who objects to preparing religious tracts that say, "Jesus is the only way." A government that can force us to say things we do not believe or celebrate events that violate our beliefs has virtually unlimited power.

Those who stand for religious liberty and free speech do so on behalf of all Americans, including those with whom they disagree. And they are kind, gracious, and loving people like Jack, who was targeted not because of how he treated customers, but because of his faith.

Radical activists would have us believe that only religious extremists or political activists end up in these legal situations, but that's not true. Jack, floral design artist Barronelle Stutzman, former Atlanta fire chief Kelvin Cochran, T-shirt designer Blaine Adamson, website designer Lori Smith, and every other client whose rights of conscience ADF defends are people who hold mainstream, reasonable, millennia-old religious beliefs. The same values that only a few short years ago made you an "average American"—beliefs that millions of Catholics, Protestants, Jews, and Muslims still cherish—can today make you a target of extremist groups all over the country...groups with the money and determination to ruin your life.

One of the striking things about Jack's story is that he did everything right and still was attacked. Jack is a dedicated, caring, selfless member of his community. He goes out of his way to serve the poor. He feeds the homeless. He created and maintains a place where people can come for refuge, for peace, for support, for help. He graciously serves and genuinely respects everyone who comes into his shop, no matter who they are. We've been there countless times when a "regular" has visited from off the streets. These individuals know Jack will provide a cup of coffee, a warm place to rest, a friendly conversation, and will treat them with respect. That's just who Jack is—whether he's standing behind the counter of the cake shop or in front of a television camera on *The View*.

From the moment he opened his cake shop (and not just when same-sex marriage came on the scene), he adopted a simple rule: he serves all customers but cannot design custom cakes that conflict with his core convictions. Whether Jack can create a cake is never about the customer; it's only about the message he is being asked to express. This is a policy he applies even-handedly to everyone. But once someone decided to attack him, none of that was enough.

Many Americans still believe they will be able to skate under the radar—that the efforts to restrict religious freedom, suppress free speech, and undermine our basic rights somehow won't harm them. They're convinced that if they can just stay out of the spotlight, they'll be alright. Jack's story destroys that illusion. Until that day in July 2012, Jack had never been in the spotlight—nor did he want to be in it. What has happened to him over the last eight and a half years shows that staying out of the spotlight won't be an option much longer. If we hold beliefs that run counter to the current progressive narrative about gender, sexuality, marriage, and human dignity, the spotlight can very easily turn to us. And here's food for thought: Perhaps that is precisely because so many of us have avoided the spotlight for far too long. Our silence has impaired our witness on these issues and likely helped facilitate a kind of religious intolerance unlike anything we've seen in generations.

This brings us to the final reason why it was imperative for Jack to share his story: to inspire like-minded people across the country and around the world to stand up for our beliefs. Sure, it takes courage. Perseverance. And most importantly, a strong and steady faith. And yes, Jack's story is about challenges, struggles, attacks. It is about a decent and kind man going through a very dark time without knowing whether there would be light on the other side. But the hero of Jack's story is God, who always brings light to pierce the darkness, Who has our days and moments planned from the creation of the world, and Who has brought beautiful things out of the ugliness that Jack has faced and continues to endure.

J ack's story is also about a legal battle that went to the highest court in this nation and focused on one of the most hotly contested cultural issues—whether government can brand people of faith as bigots and banish them from polite society for holding beliefs shared by millions since at least the beginning of Western civilization.

The Supreme Court's decision suggests not. *Masterpiece Cakeshop v. Colorado Civil Rights Commission* affects every American who believes that marriage is the union between one man and one woman. It has impacted artists, counselors, teachers, business owners, and ministries across the country. In its ruling, the Supreme Court did a lot more than scold Colorado for its hostility toward Jack: it reaffirmed the baseline rule that governmental hostility toward religion has no place in our society and that the government cannot selectively enforce its laws against people who take their faith seriously. The decision in Jack's case provides durable and broad protections that people of all faiths can rely on for decades to come.

To date, the decision has been referenced in more than eighty separate court cases, including others decided by the Supreme Court and even in U.S. Senate confirmation hearings for potential Supreme Court justices. The High Court first referred to the *Masterpiece* precedent just weeks after making it, when it sent Barronelle Stutzman's case back to the Washington Supreme Court for review. The state court had ruled against her and had affirmed state officials' hostility towards her religious beliefs—which included suing her in both her professional and personal capacities, threatening her savings and retirement should she lose her case. When considering whether to take it, the Supreme Court ordered the state to reconsider its decision in light of *Masterpiece's* very clear prohibition of state hostility toward religious beliefs. Since then, *Masterpiece* has also been cited to support the rights of artists (like filmmakers, photographers, and calligraphers) to create custom works consistent with their conscience, faith-based adoption agencies to place children in homes with a married mother and father, and members of a religious group to distribute food and religious literature to college students.

Masterpiece was not the only crucial case during the 2017–2018 term in which the Supreme Court affirmed religious Americans' rights to live and speak in accordance with their beliefs. In another ADF case, *National Institute of Family and Life Advocates v. Becerra*, the Court ruled that the State of California could not force pro-life pregnancy resource centers to advertise for abortion clinics, pointing out that the state cannot discriminate against licensed professionals because of their viewpoint. Writing for the majority, Justice Clarence Thomas indicated that Americans do not forfeit their personal freedoms by entering the marketplace. In his concurrence, Justice Anthony Kennedy explained that California's law was "a paradigmatic example of the serious threat presented when government seeks to impose its own message in the place of individual speech, thought, and expression." He concluded by reminding us all of a bedrock truth: "Governments must not be allowed to force persons to express a message contrary to their deepest convictions."

These are vitally important rulings from the Supreme Court. They affirm that Christians need not leave their beliefs at the door when they go to work, even if those beliefs are unpopular or go against the current cultural tide. Just like every other American, Christians have the right to work, speak, gather, and live in accordance with their deeply held convictions.

While Jack's victory has helped to protect religious liberty, what lay at stake in his case has been muted by his victory. So let us be clear: a loss would have been particularly devastating to religious liberty.

Imagine if the Supreme Court had issued a ruling that forced individuals to create art, express messages, and celebrate religious ceremonies in violation of their deepest core convictions. Imagine the fallout had the Court followed the government and ACLU's urging to label Christians and all those of Abrahamic faith traditions as engaging in bigotry and deemed them unworthy of basic First Amendment protections. These are the concerns that ADF and Jack were keenly aware of throughout this journey. The stakes were much higher than many realized.

What impressed us most during the long years of *Masterpiece* was how little all the vitriol rattled Jack. Sure, there were days when he was troubled, but it was almost always because he was concerned about those around him: his friends, his employees, and most especially his family. Jack believed from the very beginning that God would take care of him—and from that solid ground he could turn his attention to caring for those around him.

It is tempting to try to draw easy morals from these kinds of stories when reality is often more complicated. But from Jack's story, the moral is right there for us to see: When you stand firm on God's enduring promises, He will not let you down. The victory may not always be what you thought when you started, but He promises to use all circumstances for our good and His glory.

Acknowledgments

I cannot begin to acknowledge everyone who has been instrumental in the creation and development of this book, this "memoir." But if not for the help of my friend Sealy Yates, none of it would have taken shape at all. No book, no story, no nothing. He has helped me from the start, coaching me, encouraging me, planning everything. Even defending me in court!

And while Sealy was responsible for believing in the possibility of my story becoming a book, he also helped to connect me with two very helpful and talented writers who did all the heavy lifting in making my story come to life: John Sloan and Chris Potts. Many thanks also to Karla Dial at Salem Books for her expertise in editing the many pages (and giving me some fun grammar lessons to boot!).

I also cannot neglect to mention the immeasurable help from everyone at Alliance Defending Freedom! They came to my aid within the first few days of this battle and have stood beside me every step of the way: Nicolle, Kristen, Jeremy, Kerri, Jake, Jon, Kate, Jim Campbell, Bob Trent, Kellie, Caleb, Matt, Michael Farris, and Alan Sears. (Sorry, but there are too many more to single out by name!)

But besides all these wonderful people, Masterpiece itself would not have survived the first three weeks or months, let alone almost three decades of business, without the generous help of close friends and family. Terry and Trish, your tireless efforts, patience with me when cakes aren't ready to deliver, or the mess I've just made in the back... Vivian, what can I say? You have quietly taken it upon yourself to make this place shine! Linda and Jim, when I didn't have the money to match my dreams, you've been there, not only with the physical, tangible help, but also with the spiritual example of what God has designed us to do for brothers in Christ.

Lastly (since there isn't space here to write a "book" simply to thank people, and I have to keep this short), thanks to everyone else who has helped me and Debi in any way. I hope you know who you are.

Finally, thanks also to my two best friends in the whole wide world: Lee, who can build or fix anything (and did so right here in the cakeshop many, many times), and Brian, whose humor, competitive spirit, and decorating skills are without equal. None of this happened without you.

I love you all!!

Jack Phillips

Notes

Prologue

1. Matthew 10:16.
2. Matthew 10:18–20.
3. "Now there are also many other things that Jesus did. Were every one of them to be written, I suppose that the world itself could not contain the books that would be written" (John 21:25 ESV).
4. John 20:30–31 NIV.
5. Acts 26:28–29.

Chapter 6: My Dream Girl

1. "It is not good for the man to be alone; I will make a helper suitable for him" (Genesis 2:18 NIV).

Chapter 7: Meeting God

1. Daniel 8:17.
2. Acts 9:5; 22:8; 26:15.
3. Luke 1:38, 46–47 NASB.
4. Romans 6:23.
5. Ephesians 2:4.
6. John 3:16 KJV.
7. 1 Timothy 1:15 NIV.
8. "For God did not send His Son into the world to condemn the world, but to save the world through Him" (John 3:17 NIV).
9. Mark 2:7 NIV.
10. Philippians 2:6–8.
11. Hebrews 4:15.
12. John 3:7 ESV.
13. "It is for freedom that Christ has set us free, stand firm therefore and do not let yourselves be burdened again by a yoke of slavery [to sin]" (Galatians 5:1: NIV).
14. "For it is by grace you have been saved, through faith—and this not from yourselves, it is the gift of God—not by works, so that no one can boast" (Ephesians 2:8–9 NIV).

15.   "For if you confess with your mouth, 'Jesus is Lord,' and believe in your heart that God raised Him from the dead, you will be saved. For it is with your heart that you believe and are justified, and it is with your mouth that you confess and are saved" (Romans 10:9–10: NIV).

16.   "For we are God's masterpiece.... He has created us anew in Christ Jesus, so we can do the good things He planned for us long ago...." (Ephesians 2:10: NLT). (I like the NLT's translation of the Greek word *poiema*, often translated "workmanship," but a word we often use for such beautiful concepts as "poetry" and translated here as "masterpiece.")

Chapter 8: Gaining Experience, Gaining Wisdom

1.   The site gotquestions.org notes at least 169 Bible verses in which God promises to provide for us.

2.   Ephesians 6:4 NASB.

3.   Deuteronomy 6:7.

4.   3 John 1:4 NIV.

Chapter 9: Opening the Shop

1.   I don't remember everyone who was in the shop that morning to see what happened, but Debi and all three of my kids were there, as well as my sister Linda, her husband, Jim, and their five kids.

2.   Nearly thirty years later, Rod is still a customer.

Chapter 12: The Thing about Weddings

1.   Genesis 2 NIV.

2.   Matthew 19:4–6; Mark 10:6–9.

Chapter 13: Taking On the Government

1.   1 Corinthians 6:7.

2.   Romans 13:1–2, 7 NIV.

3.   Daniel 2:21 NIV.

4.   Philippians 4:6–7.

5.   Matthew 22:21.

6.   Romans 13:8.

Chapter 15: Cruelty and Contempt

1. Alliance Defending Freedom, "Revealed: Colo. Commissioner Compared Cake Artist to Nazi," News & Media, January 12, 2015, http://www.adfmedia.org/News/PRDetail/9479.

Chapter 22: Victory

1. This story is recorded in the Old Testament in Daniel 3 NIV.
2. Proverbs 21:1.

Chapter 28: Lessons Learned

1. Genesis 50:19–20.
2. Psalm 76:10.
3. James 5:10–11.
4. Romans 14:7.
5. 1 Peter 3:14–15 NIV.
6. James 1:2–4.
7. John 20:30–31 NIV.